WORD 6

Oxford Computer Training

GW00600682

Hodder & Stoughton

A MEMBER OF THE HODDER HEADLINE GROUP

Acknowledgements

A number of products have been referred to in this book, many of which are registered trademarks. These are acknowledged as being the property of their owners.

The trademarks mentioned in this book include:

Microsoft: Windows, MS-DOS, Word for Windows 6, Excel 5, Access.

IBM: PC

Intel: i486, Pentium

Alice in Wonderland was written by Lewis Carroll.

The Owl and the Pussycat was written by Edward Lear.

British Library Cataloguing in Publication Data

ISBN 0 340 63944 X

First published 1995
Impression number 10 9 8 7 6 5 4 3 2 1
Year   1999 1998 1997 1996 1995

Typeset by Oxford Computer Training.
Printed in Great Britain for Hodder & Stoughton Educational, a division of Hodder Headline Plc, 338 Euston Road, London NW1 3BH by Cox & Wyman, Reading, Berks.

CONTENTS

List of Contributors

Ross Bentley, Jon Collins, Ian Cunningham, Shona McLeod, Andrew O'Connell, Gary Powell, Brian Reid, Julie Robertson, Narinderpal Singh Thethi, Pamela Stanworth, Donald Taylor, John Ward, Hugh Simpson-Wells, Wendy Tagg, Duncan Young

'I'm sure those are not the right words,'
said poor Alice, and her eyes filled with tears.

Alice in Wonderland

1

— INTRODUCTION —

This chapter covers:
- Conventions used in this book.
- The aims of this book.

Welcome

This book is intended for first time users of Microsoft Word for Windows version 6.0. References to 'Word' should be taken to mean Word version 6.0; any references to earlier versions will include the version number explicitly. It is assumed that you have a working knowledge of Windows. If you do not, read the companion book *Teach Yourself Windows*.

This book provides the user with a basic understanding of the operation of Word. It starts by introducing some basic word processing concepts and how to create simple, but professional looking letters. It covers many of the advantages of using a wordprocessor within Windows, such as being able to see on the screen exactly what you see on paper, and goes on to use some of Word's simpler features including the storage of copies of your text on file and the ability to undo any mistakes you make.

This book is not a definitive source of information, and as such it is not to be taken as an authoritative document; it is merely a guide which will help to introduce you to Word and supplement its manual.

——————————— **Conventions** ———————————

Throughout this book, instructions that you must carry out are written

🖱 *like this (in italics, with a mouse graphic to the left).*

Anything that you must type on the keyboard is written `like this.`

Key words are shown like this: **DOS**, **button**, **Toolbar**, **mouse**.

Special keys are shown like this: Ctrl, T, etc., with combinations shown as Ctrl T (which means press T whilst holding down Ctrl).

On screen 'buttons' are shown like this: OK

Enter means the enter key (also known as: carriage return, return, CR, etc.)

Space means the spacebar.

References to filenames are shown as FILENAME.DOC.

👍 *Hints and warnings about how to do things are often given in italics like this with a 'thumbs up' symbol at the start.*

> ∽ *Text appearing in a box with this graphic is usually a little technical or an aside not strictly essential to the issue under discussion. You may prefer to skip it on the first reading.*

From time to time you will see a box containing summary points which reinforce the section of text that they follow, like this:

Summary: Word for Windows 6

- This book is for new users of Word for Windows 6 ('Word'). It assumes a working knowledge of Windows.
- Instructions appear in italics. Text for you to type appears `in this style.`
- Keywords appear like this: **keyword.**
- This is a summary box, intended to reinforce the points made in the main body of the text.

2

BASIC PRINCIPLES

This chapter covers:

- The relationship between the computer, Windows, and Word for Windows 6.

- How to start Word.

What is Word?

Word is a word processing program for manipulating text and storing it on disk, with the ultimate aim of printing (editing, reprinting, etc.) a document (letter, memo, thesis, book, mailshot, etc.). Unlike many older word processors, Word is graphics-based (through the Windows environment); it shows your work largely as it will be printed not only from the point of view of text attributes (bold, italics, typefaces, etc.) and positioning, but also including pictures, tables and text.

———————— What is Windows? ————————

Microsoft Windows is a program that acts as a 'user interface' between you and your computer's Disk Operating System (DOS). With Windows a user can work with several programs (or 'applications') simultaneously. It also provides an easy means of transferring information between applications. You could say that Windows provides services for applications like Word and Excel to use.

———————— What is an application? ————————

An application is a computer program designed to perform a particular task. Windows provides an operating environment under which a number of applications programs can run.

Windows comes with a number of standard applications, and a variety of other Windows applications can be purchased, e.g. Excel (a spreadsheet tool), Word (a word processor and the subject of this book) and Access (a database). There are also many applications that are not specifically designed to run in the Windows environment. Such 'DOS' or 'non-Windows' applications can also be run from Windows.

Windows applications all make use of the Windows graphical environment in a standard way, allowing you to transfer skills (and data) between applications. This means that many of the skills and even everyday keystrokes are the same in most Windows applications, so that when you have learnt to use one Windows application you are already well on the way to mastering others. This approach is known as the Common User Interface (CUI).

Windows also allows you to load more than one application at the same time, and makes switching between them easy.

If you are using an 80386 or higher processor, you can even have several applications running at once.

Starting Word

Starting from the Program Manager

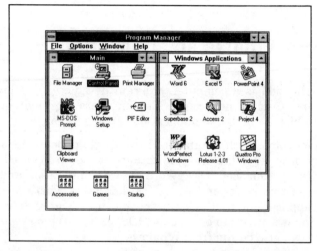

Typically, when you start Windows, the Program Manager will present a number of groups of programs and accessories, one of which might be 'Word 6' or 'Microsoft Office' and include the Word icon.

 Word can be loaded in the usual way (by double-clicking the icon). You may have a different set-up but in any case you can load Word by choosing File Run and typing (typically) WINWORD.

An application can usually be loaded directly from the DOS command line by typing the name of the program after the command to load Windows, e.g. **WIN WINWORD**. In such a case, the Program Manager will be loaded and iconized and Word will be presented as active.

Pre-loading Word

It is possible to arrange for applications to be loaded automatically on starting Windows, either as icons or as windows. On your system, Word may load automatically. If this is the case, use the copy that is already loaded (either already on screen or iconized) and avoid loading another copy: i.e. don't double-click the icon in the Program Manager.

 The simplest way of pre-loading (or running) Word is to put the Word icon into the Startup group in Windows. Word will then run automatically when you load Windows.

Tip of the day

The first thing you see on loading Word is the Tip of the Day:

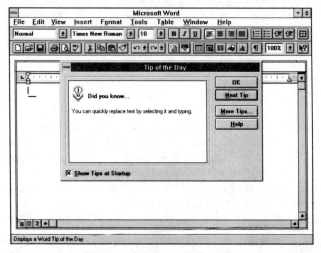

These tips are (usually) helpful suggestions. Every time you start Word you will be presented with a new tip, unless you uncheck the ⊠ Show Tips at Startup checkbox.

🖑 *Click* ▭ OK ▭ *to close the dialog.*

Summary: Methods for starting Word

You can choose any of these options:
- Double-click 𝒲 in Program Manager, or
- Type **WIN WINWORD** at the DOS prompt (if Word is in your DOS path), or
- Double-click a Word document from within the File Manager, or
- Use File Run from the Program Manager menu and type WINWORD, or
- If so configured, Windows and Word may load automatically on switching on, or
- If so configured, loading Windows may automatically load Word either full screen or as an icon.

3

THE WORD ____ SCREEN

This chapter covers:
- Word as it first appears when started.
- Standard Windows features: the maximise and mini-mise buttons; the title bar; moving the insertion point by using scroll bars and by moving the document.
- The menu bar.
- Right-click shortcut menus.
- The status bar.
- Toolbars: ToolTips and help messages; buttons as menu shortcuts; moving toolbars.
- The mouse pointer.
- The insertion point ('cursor'): moving it using the mouse pointer and keyboard.
- The end of document marker.
- The ruler: showing and hiding it.

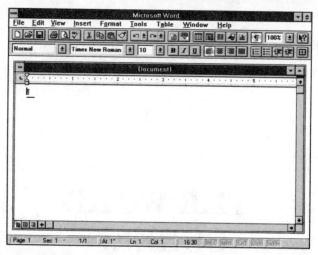

This is the default screen (as it comes 'out of the box'). Depending upon the configuration of your computer and the options chosen by the last user, your screen might look different.

If the Word window is not occupying the whole of the screen and you wish it to do so:

Maximise the Word window by clicking ▲ in the Word application window.

The application window is the window that contains the whole of the Word program. It can be dragged to any part of the screen when not maximised and can contain other windows called document windows. Document windows, when not maximised can only be dragged within an application window. Each window will have its own title bar and can be sized independently of other windows.

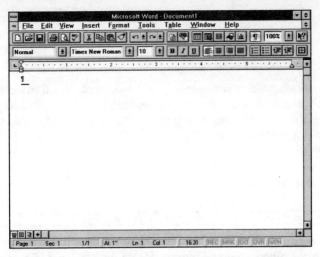

If the document window is occupying the whole of the screen as shown, and you wish to return to something like the first screen above:

🖰 *Restore the document window by clicking the lower of the two restore buttons* 🔽 *at the top right-hand corner of the Word application window.*

—— **Standard Windows features** ——

Title bars

The title bar includes the name of the current document, if the document window is maximised. If you have several documents open for editing, each can have its own window with its own title bar containing the name of the document. When you have one document maximised, its name appears in the Word title bar. From here you can restore the window with the document window's 🔼 and maximise it again with the document window's 🔼. Restoring a document window allows you to see any other document windows you may also have open, though in this case there is only one open at present.

Since you have not yet named your document, Word gives it the default name of Document1. Subsequent new documents created during this session would be given starting names of Document2, Document3, etc.

The menu bar

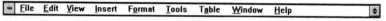

The menu bar is the horizontal strip immediately below the title bar. It has nine pull-down menus (File, Edit, etc.) in addition to the document window's control menu (when the document window is maximised). Many menu options are similar to those found in other Windows applications. In this book, you will probably be surprised to see how little use is made of the menus. Word allows you to access its most commonly used features in more convenient ways, such as using buttons in the toolbar or right-clicking to show shortcut menus (both discussed below).

To use a menu, you have two options. The first is to click the left button of the mouse over the menu title in the menu bar; the titles File and Insert are two of the possibilities. The second choice is to use the keyboard in conjunction with the ⎓Alt⎓ key. Pressing ⎓Alt⎓ and the letter underlined in the menu title will also pull down its respective menu. For example, ⎓Alt⎓⎓V⎓ will pull down the View menu.

> ☞ ⎓Alt⎓⎓Space⎓ *will pull down the Control Menu.*

The mouse pointer

When working with Word, the normal Windows mouse pointer ⬚ changes into one of several other pointers, depending on its position in the window. For example, the I-beam Ⅰ appears in the editing area, and is used to position the insertion point (see below); the right-pointing mouse pointer ⤢ appears in the **selection bar** on the left-hand side of the window. As you will see later on, the I-beam pointer is 'aware' of the type of text it is moving over. It will change to a slanted version when moving over italicised text to make selecting text easier.

The status bar

The status bar is displayed at the bottom of the document window. It gives either information about the document (position of the cursor, current page number, line number and a clock, etc.) or information about the current menu selection.

> ☞ *The status bar can also be switched off to make more space. If you haven't got a status bar, select Options... from the Tools menu. When the dialog appears, select the View tab, check ⊠ Status bar (i.e. click the status bar check box until it has a cross in it), then click* [**OK**] *. The status bar should now be visible. Similarly, the horizontal and vertical scroll bars may be turned on or off.*

——————— The toolbars ———————

Below the menu bar are the Standard toolbar and the Formatting toolbar (called the 'ribbon' in Word 2). You will find that many of the most commonly used commands can be accessed with only a mouse-click or two. The actions the buttons perform can also be accomplished in other (usually longer but more detailed) ways; so the toolbars offer what are best thought of as frequently used shortcuts.

> You can change how the toolbar buttons look, what they do and on which toolbar the buttons appear, through the <u>C</u>ustomize... command on the <u>T</u>ools menu, but it is better to use the pre-set toolbars until you are more experienced with Word.

When you need to do something, look in the toolbar first. The picture on the buttons gives a very good clue to what each does, and if that doesn't help, you can use the ToolTips, which appear as you move the cursor across the toolbars.

Position the mouse pointer over 🖻 *and wait for a moment.*

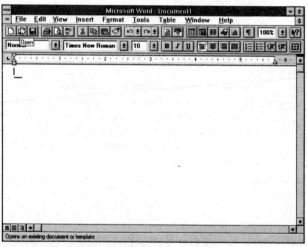

The yellow ToolTip Open in conjunction with the help line on the status bar, should be enough to tell you that the button is the file open button. This button is a shortcut for the <u>F</u>ile <u>O</u>pen command.

Try looking at some other ToolTips by positioning the mouse pointer over the buttons.

Click 📂

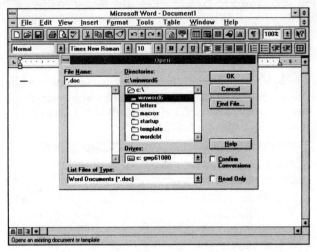

☝ *Dialogs can be moved by dragging the title bar with the mouse; dialogs usually have an OK button* `OK` *and a cancel button* `Cancel`. *If you get the wrong dialog by mistake just click* `Cancel`.

The same dialog is also available from the menu.

 Click `Cancel` *to close the dialog and choose* Open *from the* File *menu.*

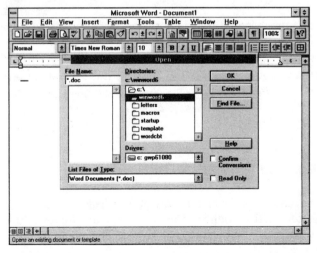

You can see that this is exactly the same dialog that you saw a moment ago. You are going to use this dialog to open a demonstration document. When opening a file you must first select the directory where the file is stored. File storage will be covered in more detail later, but for now:

🖰 *Double-click* 🗀 WORDCBT. *Then double-click the file* SAMPLE10.DOC *in the File Name list. (If the Open dialog doesn't immediately display* 🗀 WINWORD *you may have to find your way to* 🗀 WINWORD *first.)*

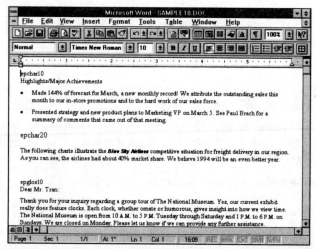

This document is one that is supplied by Microsoft as a learning tool. You are going to use it in the exercise that follows.

> ✐ *This document was created by Microsoft and comes shipped with Word as a sample file. The 'epchar' codes are only for use as part of a computer based training package and can be ignored in this context.*

Moving the toolbars

Toolbars can be positioned in any of four fixed positions or 'docks': top, bottom, left or right of the Word window. Further, they may be left 'floating' at a position you choose. The advantage of floating toolbars is that you have more space available on screen as the shape of the toolbar cannot reduce the document area.

🖱 *Click the background of the toolbar, hold the mouse button down and drag the toolbar to the middle of the screen.*

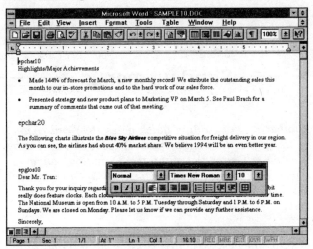

To dock a toolbar (fix it to an edge of the screen), drag it to the side of the screen until the grey outline changes to a longer bar.

🖱 *Try docking the toolbar on the left edge of the screen.*

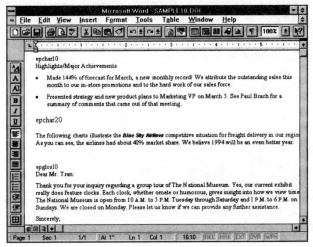

The position of the toolbar is a question of convenience and your choice may depend on what other toolbars you might be using.

For the moment, drag the Formatting toolbar away from its dock on the left hand side of the screen and dock it at the top of the screen once more.

Shortcut menus

Another way of gaining quick access to Word commands is by using the short-cut menus. These are activated by right-clicking (clicking the right mouse button) an area of the screen. The menu displayed depends upon the area that the mouse pointer is over at the time of right-clicking.

Position the mouse pointer I over some text and right-click.

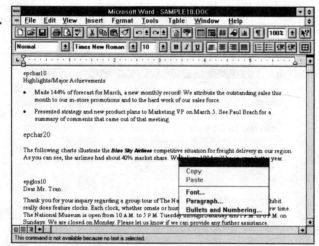

We will look more at this menu later when we consider formatting methods. For the time being close the menu by right-clicking the text again (**not** the menu), or pressing [Esc] on the keyboard.

—— Moving around a document ——

The insertion point

The flashing vertical line in your text is the insertion point (often referred to as the 'cursor'). This line marks the position at which any text you type will be entered.

🖱 *Try moving the insertion point by clicking various places in the document. You can also move it with the cursor keys.*

👍 Hint: A common mistake is to move the I-beam Ⅰ to where you'd like to insert text and then forget the click to position the insertion point. You will end up entering text somewhere else.

Some insertion point movement keystrokes	
`Home`	moves to the beginning of the current line
`End`	moves to the end of the current line
`PgUp`	moves one screen up
`PgDn`	moves one screen down
`Ctrl` `Home`	moves to the beginning of the current document
`Ctrl` `End`	moves to the end of the current document
`Ctrl` `PgUp`	moves to the top of the screen
`Ctrl` `PgDn`	moves to the bottom of the screen
`Ctrl` `←`	moves one word to the left
`Ctrl` `→`	moves one word to the right
`Ctrl` `↑`	moves to the beginning of the previous paragraph
`Ctrl` `↓`	moves to the beginning of the next paragraph

Practise using these keystrokes now by moving the insertion point around the document.

Afterwards, press Ctrl End *to move the insertion point to the end of the document.*

The end of document marker

The thick horizontal line (▬) at the left hand margin shows the bottom of the document. This marker is only visible in normal view (if you are in any doubt about which view you are seeing, you could switch to normal view by selecting Normal from the View menu). Notice that you cannot use the mouse pointer to move the insertion point beyond the end of the document.

 Try moving the insertion point beyond the end of the document.

The scroll bars

The scroll bars appear to the right hand side and the bottom of the screen, as is usual in most Windows applications. They are used to assist you in moving around your document in both the up and down direction (vertical scroll bar) and the left to right direction (horizontal scroll bar) There are three ways of using them:

- clicking an arrow button at the end of a scroll bar, thus moving the document a small amount in the appropriate direction;
- clicking the scroll bar above or below the scroll box, moving the document a screenful at a time;
- dragging the scroll box, moving the document by a controllable amount.

The distinction between moving the document and moving the insertion point should be made clear.

 Move the insertion point to the top of the document (hint: Ctrl Home *). Now drag the vertical scroll box to the bottom of the scroll bar.*

Notice that when you scroll the contents of the window, the insertion point does not move across the text. In this case, it stayed at the top of the document even though that was not visible.

The Ruler

The ruler allows you to set and manipulate tabs, indents, margins and table column widths (amongst other things). These functions will be examined later.

The Ruler can be switched on and off from the View menu.

 If the ruler is not visible, switch the Ruler on from the View menu.

Summary: The Word screen

- **Title bar:** there is one for Word and one for each open document. These are combined if the document is maximised.
- **Menu bar:** this contains the Word menus.
- **Toolbars:** these give access to most of the commonly-used shortcuts.
- **Ruler**: this displays and controls tabs and indenting, among other things.
- **Toolbars and ruler:** these can be hidden to increase the display area (from the View menu).
- **Status bar:** this shows various pieces of information (and can be hidden from Tools Options...).
- **Scroll bars:** these work as expected and can be hidden to increase the display area (from Tools Options...).
- I: I-beam, used to position the insertion point in text.
- **Insertion point:** this is the flashing vertical line that marks the position in the document where text will be entered.
- ▬ : this is the end of document marker.

4

A SIMPLE LETTER

This chapter covers:

- Entering text.
- Wordwrap.
- Correct use of `Enter` and `Space`.
- Paragraph markers.
- Insert and Overtype – the `Insert` key.

In this section, you will type a letter, short enough to fit on one page.

Start a new document by clicking 🖳 *or by using the* New *command on the* File *menu.*

Using the New command in the File menu will produce a dialog containing a series of options leading to opening one of the many templates. These templates are supplied with Word and provide standard starting documents.

> 🖘 *Some templates have special facilities known as macros included to help you create your document.*

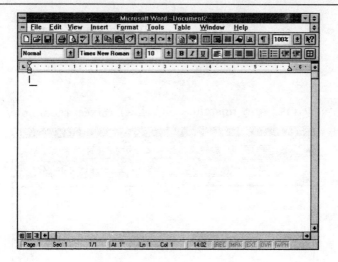

—————————— Creating the letter ——————————

Entering text

You are about to write a letter to someone. You can choose the recipient of the letter or use the example below; but assume that you are using headed notepaper, so you don't need to type your own address.

🖰 *Type in the address of the recipient, pressing ⌨Enter at the end of each line.*

If you make a mistake and you happen to realise straightaway, use ⌫ to delete it, then carry on. If you notice a mistake further back, leave it; you will correct it later. Typically, you might type:

Mr	E	Type-Jaguar	Enter
14	Acacia	Ave	Enter
Kennington			Enter
Oxford			Enter
Oxon Enter			

If you've made any mistakes (as below), correct them now.

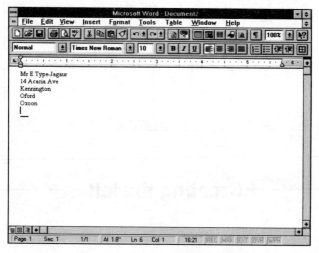

🖰 *Try to correct your mistakes. Use the four arrow keys to move the insertion point to the mistake. Then use either ⌫, which deletes to the left or* Del*, which deletes to the right and correct your errors.*

You will remember that you can position the insertion point simply by clicking at the appropriate position in the document.

You should find that typing characters in the middle of a word simply causes them to be inserted at the insertion point. If you find that you overwrite existing characters as you type, you need to press the ⎀ key on your keyboard (see page 33).

🐭 *Now move to the bottom of your text by pressing* ⌨️Ctrl ⌨️End *or by simply clicking at the bottom of the document.*

You need some space before the next item of text. It is tempting to press the ⌨️↓ key to try to make some space, but this doesn't work because there is nowhere to go down to (yet).

Word provides you with, to all intents and purposes, an infinitely stretchable piece of paper, but it only builds it as necessary. If you were to fill the screen with spaces by holding down the space bar, you *could* move about all over the place with the arrow keys. This is not only a waste of time and computer memory, but very bad practice as you will understand once you are proficient in Word.

You should make certain that you understand the difference between a space and nothing! Nothing is what fills the screen to start with; it also lies at the end of your document and you can't move into it. A space is a character (character is computer jargon for a letter, number, symbol, etc. like A, x or 5), and although by default you can't actually see it on the screen, Word treats a space just like any other character most of the time.

So how could the space you require be made? Well, how did you start a new line after each line of the address?

🐭 *Press* ⌨️Enter *several times.*

Then press ⌨️←Back *several times to remove the empty lines.*

You should see that ⌨️Enter is another character, similar to ⌨️Space, and that you can insert and delete it even though you can't (normally) see it.

🐭 *Type* ⌨️Enter *a few times until you have a space between the address and the start of the letter, then type:*

Dear Edward,⌨️Enter⌨️Enter

Your screen should now look something like this:

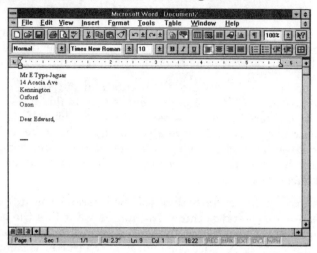

If your screen doesn't look quite the same, use the arrow keys, ⌫Back and Del, and type the necessary characters to correct it.

Note that the status bar at the bottom of the screen has changed to indicate that your insertion point has moved down the page. You should have noticed that the **At**, **Ln** and **Col** counters changed whilst you typed each line.

> *The Col value simply refers to the number of characters between the start of the line and the insertion point. Since, in most typefaces, characters are not all the same size, Col 20, for example, on one line may well be at a completely different horizontal position to Col 20 on the next.*

Next, you are going to type a paragraph. This sounds simple enough, but in fact introduces one of the most important concepts of word processing: wordwrap.

Start typing the text below (but don't press Enter *until the end of the paragraph.)*

The text is as follows:

> 'The time has come', the Walrus said, 'to talk of many things, Of shoes and ships and sealing wax, of cabbages and kings; Of why the sea is boiling hot and whether pigs have wings!'

You will discover that if a word that you type won't fit on the end of the current line, Word moves it onto the next line. The result might look like this:

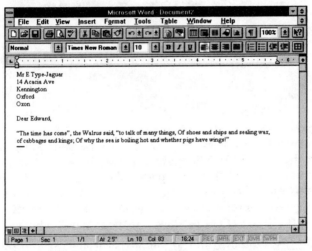

This action is known as wordwrap. You could, perhaps, imagine the line wrapping around the back of the screen and reappearing on the other side or 'pushing the word onto the next line'. Word is said to have 'wrapped' the lines in the paragraph. You have put a **paragraph mark** at the end of the paragraph by pressing Enter which tells Word to end the line straightaway. Pressing Enter again inserts a blank line to separate the paragraphs.

The show/hide button

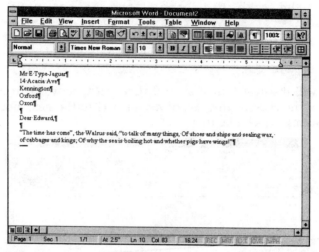

🖰 *Click* ¶ *near the right end of the Standard toolbar while watching the screen.*

You can now see all the paragraph marks and spaces in the document (if there were any tab characters, you would be able to see them as well). The ends of paragraphs are indicated by paragraph marks (¶) and spaces show up as dots between words. Notice also that the ¶ button on the Standard toolbar now appears depressed, letting you know that the special characters are currently being 'shown' rather than 'hidden'.

Press Ctrl Home to move to the top of the document and compare carefully the address and the 'paragraph' you have just typed.

You should see a paragraph mark at the end of every line in the address, but in the main body of the letter, there is only a single mark at the end of the 'paragraph'. This is correct, as you want to force each part of the address to be on a different line (using Enter), but you can leave Word to arrange the lines of the paragraphs neatly, which saves you from the agonies familiar to typewriter users, of decisions about words near the ends of lines.

Altering text

It is useful for you to see why it is important to let Word break the lines of paragraph text for you instead of your putting in paragraph markers:

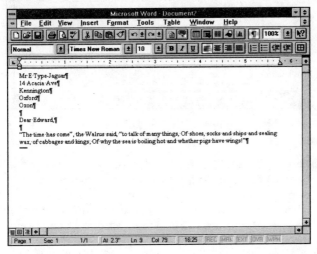

🖰 *Move down into the paragraph and insert, after 'shoes',* ⌷ Space *socks.*

Notice that Word automatically inserts new text when you type within existing text; the new text is inserted at the insertion point, forcing the existing text to move along to the right.

Notice also how the whole paragraph was reformatted to accommodate the extra word and how the words were wrapped. This would not have happened if there were paragraph markers everywhere. The following screen shows what would have happened if paragraph marks had originally been used at the end of every line:

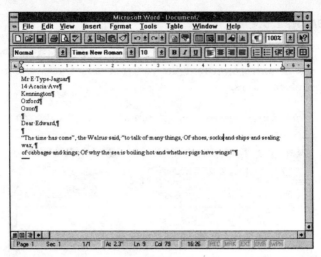

Complete the document with the following text, making use of
Enter and Space only where appropriate:

**The Owl and the Pussycat went to sea in a
beautiful pea-green boat. They took some
honey and plenty of money, wrapped up in a
five-pound note. They sailed away for a year
and a day, to the land where the bong tree
grows.**

*Now add a conventional sign-off and the sender's name
(this time, do use Enter several times to create blank lines
as needed).*

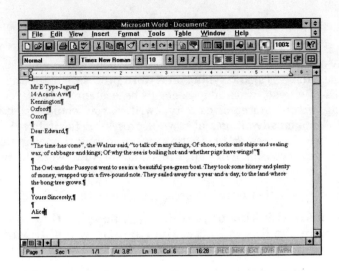

Paragraph marks

There are one or two simple rules to which you should adhere:

Enter The **Enter** key should only be used to end paragraphs. When you are typing continuous text, Word will decide where each line should end and will automatically wrap words that do not fit on one line onto the start of the next. Whilst this may appear to be only a small advantage when you type in your text, it is an invaluable feature when you begin to edit your text, as words will also move back when more space becomes available. In this way, the line lengths remain optimal.

☞ *Enter may, of course, also be pressed after titles and on its own to produce empty lines. It is important that you recognise these as paragraphs (if you like, short paragraphs and very short paragraphs).*

Space Spaces should only be used singly to separate words and perhaps in pairs at the ends of sentences. Any other use of spaces, e.g. to lay out tables, is entirely wrong, and is not likely to produce the desired result when printed (This is a consequence of factors such as proportional character spacing, but is not something that can be discussed fully here.)

The difference between typing on a typewriter, using lots of spaces and Enter's, and typing on a word processor using the features of the software may seem to be academic. However, by using a word processor as a 'typewriter', you would forfeit one of the major advantages of a word processor: flexibility. Using your word processor like a typewriter means that you would have to retype (or edit) large portions of your work to make small changes ... just like using a typewriter.

If unsure whether or not to press Enter, follow the OCT rule:

If you are thinking of pressing Enter, imagine that the last word on the line is in fact the first. Do you still want to press Enter?

If the answer is 'Yes' then you **must** press Enter to start a new line (do not use spaces to force the insertion point onto the next line, this is even worse practice than using Enter too many times). If the answer is 'No' then just carry on typing and let Word take care of the line ending. **Do not** be tempted to type spaces to get the insertion point onto the next line. It may look all right for the present but a few edits later those spaces may find themselves in the middle of a line, which would look very strange indeed!

Making and joining paragraphs

To make a piece of text into two paragraphs, position the insertion point to the left of the first letter of the first word of what is to be the second paragraph and press Enter. You can press Enter again if you want an empty line between the paragraphs. You have inserted paragraph marks.

To join two pieces of text into one paragraph, either position the insertion point after the last character (letter, punctuation mark or space) of the first paragraph and press Del until the text joins up, or position the insertion point to the left of the first letter of the second paragraph and press ←Back until the paragraphs join. Use Space to insert any necessary spaces at the join. You are, in effect, deleting the paragraph markers that were separating the two paragraphs. You will be able to see this more clearly if you use the show-hide button (¶) on the standard toolbar to display the paragraph marks before you begin.

Experiment with joining and splitting paragraphs in the letter. Ensure that you end up with the proper paragraph divisions.

—————— Insert versus overtype ——————

Sometimes, it is more convenient to type over existing text that you do not wish to keep than first to delete it and then insert new text. On many wordprocessors this option is available by pressing the Insert key on your keyboard. Word provides this facility: pressing Insert will switch to overtype mode and cause **OVR** to appear highlighted in the keyboard reference area of the status bar (bottom right on the screen).

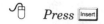 *Press* Insert

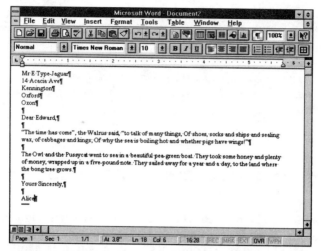

While **OVR** is displayed you will find that any text typed within the existing text will replace or 'overtype' the original text; you will also discover that the ⟵Back key no longer behaves in the same way – it removes letters and replaces them with spaces rather than deleting them entirely, leaving a gap in the text. Insert 'toggles' between the **insert mode** (the 'default') and **overtype mode**.

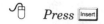 *Press* Insert *once more.*

OVR is no longer highlighted, indicating that the default insert mode is once again operative. You can switch to and from overtype mode as often as you like; use it whenever you find it convenient.

Later, you will see that there is better way of overtyping existing text, by using the typing-replaces-selection facility. In general, if you press Insert by mistake switch it off again as soon as you notice your error and use the Undo feature to correct any overtyped text (you will look more closely at Undo later).

Final checks

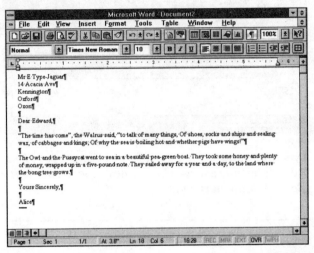

Ensure that the document looks something like the one below.

When you have finished editing your letter, but before printing it, move the insertion point as far down the document as you can: use ⬇ or click below the last line of text (or use Ctrl End). If you can move your insertion point below your last piece of text you have some unnecessary text (spaces and returns in all likelihood); these shouldn't be here, and you should ascertain why they are there so that you can try to stop this happening in future (did you press Enter several times to 'make space' after typing the last line perhaps?).

At this stage, you will now save your letter.

🖰 *Click the save button* 🖫 *on the Standard toolbar.*

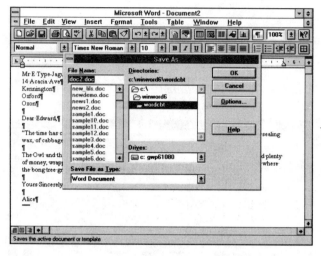

🖰 *Type the name* JAGLET *and click* [OK] *Then, from the* *F*ile *menu, choose* *C*lose *(these operations will be explained in the next chapter).*

Summary: Producing a simple letter

- Word **wordwraps** text, so that you can simply type and let Word deal with the placement of line breaks.
- Enter should only be used at the ends of paragraphs. It produces paragraph markers like this ¶.
- The Show/Hide button ¶ may be used to display non-printing characters like tab (→),paragraph marks (¶) and spaces.
- You can toggle between Insert and Overtype modes by pressing Insert
- In Overtype mode, **OVR** appears in the status bar.

5

SAVING DOCUMENTS

This chapter covers:

- Saving documents: specifying name, directory and drive.
- AutoSave.
- Different views of the document.
- Printing the document.
- Creating new documents.
- Handling multiple documents.
- Closing a document.
- Quitting Word.

At this point, you probably still have the document SAMPLE10.DOC open and displayed on the screen (it was originally opened in Chapter 3).

🖱 *If necessary, open* SAMPLE10.DOC *or pull down the* <u>Win</u>*dow menu and click on* SAMPLE10.DOC *to display it again if it is open but not active.*

🖱 *If you have just re-opened* SAMPLE10.DOC, *make a few changes to the text so that your copy differs from the version that is saved on your disk.*

👍 Having finished editing the document, it is usually a good idea to save it before printing it.

Saving a document using the save button

🖱 *Click* ⬛ *in the Standard toolbar and watch the status bar at the bottom of the screen.*

Since this document already has a name (SAMPLE10.DOC) Word assumes that you want to save it under that name again. The status bar displays a progress message for the save. This is replaced after a few seconds by the 'ordinary' status bar.

The menu equivalent to using this button is to choose Save from the File menu. A document that already has a filename is saved using that filename, overwriting any previous version that may be on disk.

File Save As

The Save As dialog

Suppose you wish to save this same document under a different name (maybe you are in the process of editing the document and want to give someone else a current copy on which to work, or you wish to keep the original in case you mess it up completely).

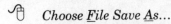 *Choose File Save As...*

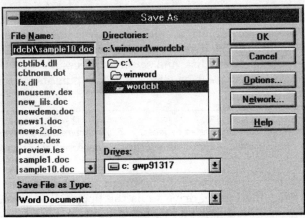

The Save <u>A</u>s dialog may look a bit complicated at first sight but it is actually quite easy to use, with a little practice. It allows you to specify a location and name under which to save a document.

Current directory

The line immediately below <u>D</u>irectories shows the way to the current directory. You need to be very conscious of which directory is the current directory because this is where your files are saved to and opened from.

The current location is shown as an MS-DOS pathname (for example, C:\WINWORD\WORDCBT, meaning the directory called WORDCBT which is contained in the directory called WINWORD which is found on drive C:).

The box in the centre of the dialog, immediately below the current directory statement, shows an indented list of the directories 'above' and 'within' the current directory. The idea behind this list is to show you a view of the directory structure 'near' the current directory and allow you to move up or down through it. See *Teach Yourself Windows* for a more detailed explanation of directory structures.

Current drive

If the directory in which you would like to work is on another drive you can change drives with the Drives list (bottom centre on the dialog). All the drives available are on the drop-down list (click ⬇ to display the list, and scroll as necessary) and you can pick the drive you want by clicking it or typing its corresponding letter.

> 👌🏻 *Drives are designated by letters A-Z. If the current location already begins with the correct drive letter it is not necessary to choose the drive.*

In the following figure, drive A: is the floppy disk drive, drive C: is the local hard disk and F: onwards are network drives.

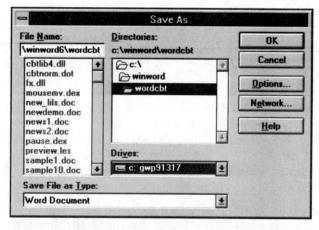

🖱 *Ensure that the correct drive is shown in the Drives list. If it isn't, pull down the Drives list and choose the drive you wish to save your documents to.*

Changing the current directory

The box below Directories: is now showing a portion of the directory structure on the C: drive. The directory structure is hierarchical and this is represented by the indenting of each

(⌷) directory symbol. Note that 📂 indicates that a directory is open.

You can change the current directory by double-clicking the directory name in the list (although you may have to scroll the list to find it). When you make a different directory current, the File Name list updates to show the documents contained in this directory. You may choose a document to open from this list. The contents of the directory structure box will also change to reflect the directories 'around' the new location. The pathname statement at the top centre of the dialog is also altered to reflect the new location.

The controls in the Save As dialog will be used to explore part of the directory structure on the disk, then return to the examples directory to save the document. Note that as you do so, the directory structure shown in these examples will probably be different from your own.

🖱 *Double-click* ⌷ C:\ *in the directory structure box.*

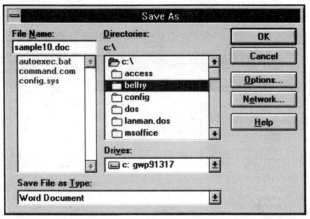

You are now in the 'root' directory of C: All the directories into which you could move are listed below ⌷ C:\ in the directory structure box. Files in the root directory are listed in the box on the left.

🖱 *Scroll down in the directory structure box to find* WINWORD *and double-click it.*

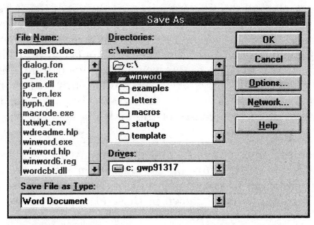

We've moved down one level in the hierarchy and are now in C:\WINWORD. Any Word files in this directory would be shown on the left.

🖱 *Double-click* WORDCBT *in the directory structure box.*

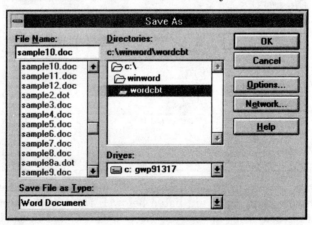

The path should now read C:\WINWORD\WORDCBT.

Giving the document a filename

After specifying a location, you need to specify a name for the file. This is done by typing a new name in the File Name box. The easiest way to do this is by double-clicking in the box (where at present it says SAMPLE10.DOC). This places the insertion point in the box and selects everything in it. Then type the new name, which will replace what was already there.

Double-click in the File Name box and type NEWSAM10

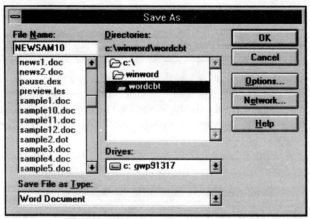

You have now specified enough information to save the file: the location to save is C:\WINWORD\WORDCBT and the file name is NEWSAM10.

Click OK *to save the file.*

You may be asked at this stage for Summary Information about the file which you are saving. It may be, therefore, that you are presented with a dialog like this:

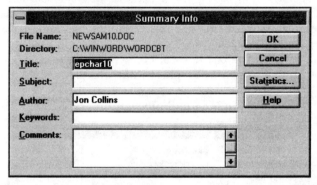

This information can be used by you or anyone else who later opens the file to give them an idea of what the file is about. You could, for instance, say in the comments field what changes you have made to the document, or what still needs to be done to it.

If you have been asked for Summary Info, add some suitable entries in these fields then click OK

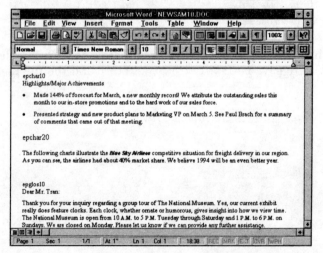

File names

Just as with non-Windows packages, you are allowed up to eight letters for a filename and an optional three letters for the extension which comes after a dot. The name should be unique in its directory. No spaces are allowed in filenames.

With Word, if you do not specify a three letter extension nor type the dot after your filename, the extension .DOC is given to it. So, although you typed NEWSAM10 earlier, the actual filename given is NEWSAM10.DOC. .DOC is the standard filename extension for Word documents.

Certain special characters are not allowed in filenames, including * / \ and : It is suggested that you restrict your filenames to normal letters and numbers. If you would like to simulate a space you can use the underscore (_) character which looks much like a space, as in MR_JONES.DOC.

Save As and Open dialogs

You may have noticed that the Save As dialog has much the same layout as the Open dialog which you used earlier to locate and open a document on disk. You will find that they are used in very much the same way for moving between directories and drives, and this is similar for many Windows programs.

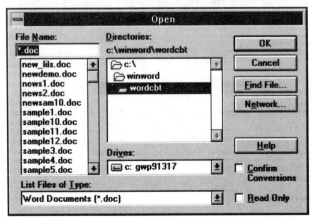

——— Saving a new document ———

If you create a new document you will need to save it. Choosing either Save or Save As from the File menu will take you to the Save As dialog where you will be able to specify a drive, directory and filename. You will try this later.

——————— Autosave ———————

You may prefer to have your work saved automatically at a specified interval, and you can find this option from the Save As dialog.

From the Save As dialog, click [Options...].

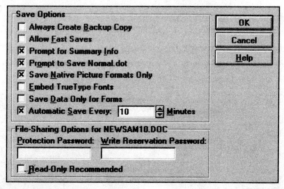

This takes you to the Save portion of the Options tabbed dialog. If ⊠ Automatic Save every *n* minutes is selected, then a copy of your document will be saved with a temporary name at the interval you specify.

The **autosaved** documents can be used to recover your work after a crash or power failure. If you quit Word in an orderly fashion, these temporary files are deleted; if you leave the program in a disorderly way, temporary files will be found next time you run Word.

👍 *Autosave is no substitute for saving the document normally (as described above)*

> ☞ *It is a very good idea to keep a backup (a 'reserve' copy in case things go wrong) of all your work. You may be fortunate in working on a network where work is regularly backed up for you. If not, you can save copies of work onto a floppy disk using File Save As... in Word.*

Summary: Saving your work

- **Save your work often!** Your edited document is stored in computer memory and is therefore susceptible to power failures and other computer crashes until it is saved. Saving your document copies it to non-volatile ('permanent') disk storage where it is safer.

- **File Save** or the 🖫 button saves your document, overwriting any previous version with the same name; its frequent use is recommended.

- **File Save As...** allows you to save a new document under a name of your choice, or to save an existing document under another name, leaving the original file intact. When you save a file, use the Save As dialog to specify the drive and directory where you want it to be stored.

- **Filenames can have up to 8 characters** (the extension .DOC is added automatically by default). Letters and numbers are legal in filenames but many punctuation symbols are not.

- **Your important documents should be backed up from time to time.** (Even hard disks are not completely safe. If this is done for you, on a network for example, you should know where to go to find the backups if something does go wrong.)

- **Autosave** (from the Options button on the Save As dialog) makes a temporary copy of your work at regular intervals. This can be used to recover work after a crash, but is not a recommended substitute for saving documents in the usual way.

6

VIEWING YOUR WORK

This chapter covers:

- Magnifying and shrinking your view of the page.
- Using the page layout view to see and edit your document as it will appear when printed.
- Splitting a window so that you can see two different parts of your document in the same window.
- Viewing two or more documents at once in separate windows.
- Arranging and moving between different windows.
- Creating two windows on the same document.

You may want to see how your document will look on the page before it is printed and make any final modifications to the document as a whole. You may also want to look at different parts of the same document, or at completely different documents at the same time for cross referencing. There are many options available for viewing the document; the most commonly-used ones will be explored.

— Zoom —

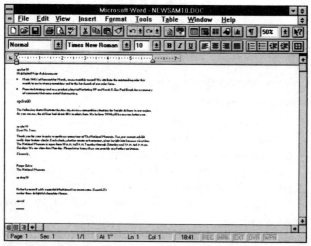 *Click the Zoom Control box at the right-hand end of the Standard toolbar.*

The list offers you a choice of zoom percentages (or you can type directly into the edit box). It can be useful to zoom to a large percentage to view small work in detail, or to zoom out to a small percentage to obtain an overview of the page.

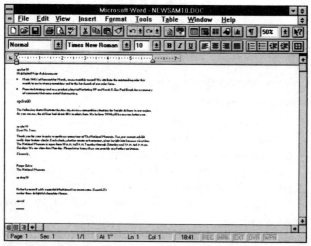 *Zoom to 50%, then try some other zoom percentages.*

Notice that the document can still be edited when you have zoomed in or out (although at small percentages it can be difficult to read the text!).

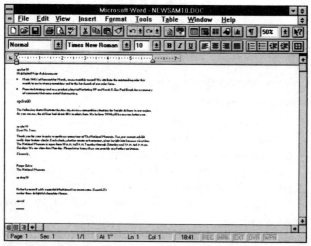 *Return to a level of zoom that shows the whole page width on the screen (choose Page Width from the Zoom control drop-down box).*

Page Layout View

Even after zooming in on a document, you cannot yet see the edges of the page on the screen. For this you can switch from normal view (which you have been using so far, by default) to page layout view.

In the bottom left corner of the Word window, you will see three small buttons. The first is probably shown depressed.

🖱 *Use <u>View</u> <u>P</u>age Layout to see the page and its edges.*

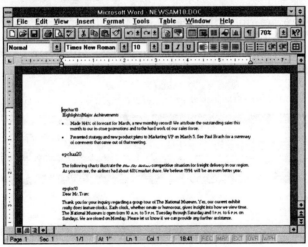

You will see that the second of the three buttons at the bottom left is now depressed. You can click these buttons to change the view instead of using the <u>V</u>iew command.

In page layout view you can see how the text is laid out on the page.

🖱 *Try out the Zoom Control again in page layout view.*

Some new options should appear now. The Two Pages option is particularly useful for longish documents, providing a view of the way the text is laid out on the pages.

New buttons also appear on the vertical scroll bar when you switch to page layout view. A little experiment with the Zoom set to Whole Page (for example) will confirm that they provide another way to move between pages of a document.

Switch back to normal view and 100% (use ▤ *at the bottom left of the screen).*

--------- **Splitting the window** ---------

If you are working with a large document, you may wish to look at different parts of your work at the same time. Word allows you to split your window into two **panes**, which can be scrolled independently.

From the Window menu, select Split

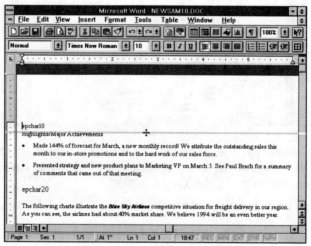

The mouse pointer turns into a horizontal split bar.

🖰 *Click at the position you want the split to be created.*

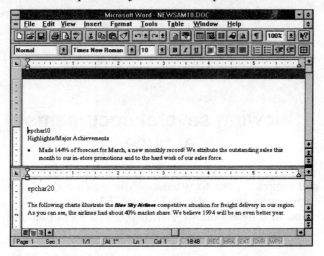

The split has created two separate panes, each with its own vertical scroll bars.

🖰 *Use the scroll bars in the lower and upper panes to satisfy yourself that they can be scrolled independently.*

Once you have created a split, you can resize it by positioning the horizontal split boundary with the mouse. To do this move the cursor over the split line (top edge of ruler). If you now drag the boundary up and down, you will see a shadow line indicating where the split will move to. To position the split, release the mouse button.

🖰 *Try this now.*

You can also remove a split once you have finished with it. You will be left with only one pane, which is the pane you are currently editing (the pane which contains the flashing cursor).

🖰 *Go to the Window menu and select Remove Split.*

Note that when the window is not split, the split boundary is represented by the wide black line above the vertical scrollbar. This can be dragged to split the window.

_____ Viewing several documents _____ at once

You will create a new document, while leaving the demonstration document open at the same time. The new document will be created in a new window, hence you will have two document windows open together.

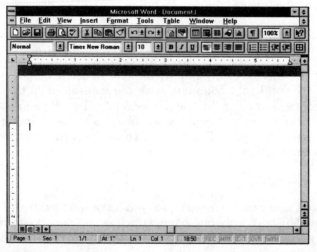

🖰 *Click ▢ in the toolbar to create a new document.*

You should now be looking at a new blank document to which Word has given the (temporary) name DOCUMENT*x* (where *x* is a number like 1 or 5, etc.).

🖰 *Type a few words into the new document, such as* **This is a new document.**

Now that you've got two documents open at the same time (the demonstration document is still open, but you just can't see it at the moment), let's cover some of the basics about working with multiple documents.

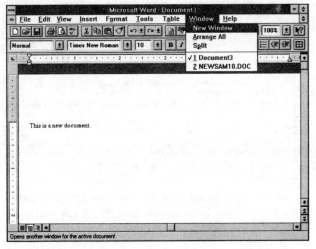 *Click the Window menu.*

This demonstrates a very useful feature of Word (and most Windows applications): at the bottom of the Window menu there is a list of all the documents that are currently open, with √ next to the active document.

Select the document on the <u>W</u>indow menu that does <u>not</u> have ✔ next to it.

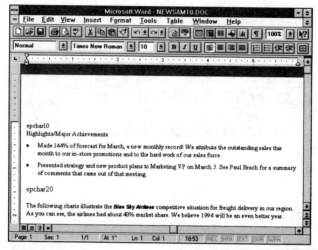

This document should now be the active document (it is now the one you can see). This is one way in which you can switch back and forth between the (many) documents that could be open at one time.

Sometimes, however, you would like to see both (all) the documents that are open – maybe you want to refer to one document while typing in another. Of course, you could resize and move both the windows until they were arranged conveniently, but this could be time-consuming. The <u>A</u>rrange All option on the <u>W</u>indow menu neatly accomplishes exactly that.

Select <u>A</u>rrange All from the <u>W</u>indow menu.

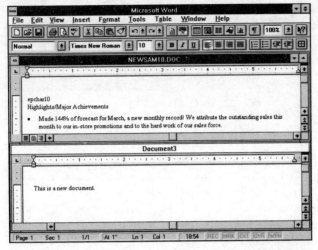

You now see both (all) the open documents on screen at once, each in its own window. <u>A</u>rrange All displays the appropriate number of windows, depending on the number of open documents.

Each document has its own scroll bars, and each has its own ruler showing the current settings in that document; but there is only one status bar for all documents. You will see later that you can also cut and paste text between windows. You can make a different window active for typing and editing simply by clicking its title bar, or by selecting its name from the <u>W</u>indow menu. The current window is indicated by the title bar showing the active title bar colour as selected in the Windows Control Panel.

The active document, as with all active windows in Windows, has a differently-coloured title bar. You can scroll around the active window without disturbing any others, and you can maximise any window (click ▲ on the right of the title bar) to make editing it easier.

Make the non-active document active by clicking its title bar.

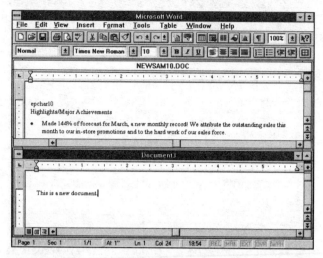

Click ▲ in the active window to maximise it.

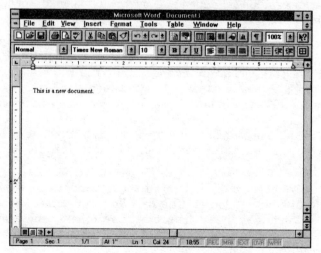

— Two windows for one document —

You can create a new window on a document which can then be manipulated exactly as if it was a window for a different document. The only difference is that changes in one of the windows will be reflected straight away in the other (since you are still looking at the same document).

🖰 *Select New Window from the Window menu.*

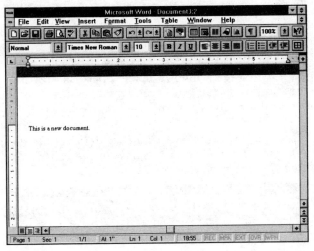

Note that the window title now says Document3:2, to indicate that it is the second of two windows on the document.

Activate the <u>W</u>indow menu and select <u>A</u>rrange All.

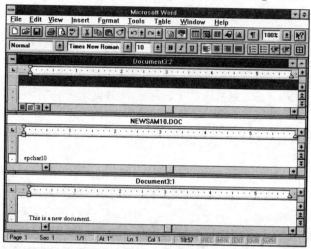

You now have three windows open. Space is starting to get somewhat cramped. You have seen how to create a second window on a document: now you will see how to close it.

Click the `Document3:2` title bar. Activate the document window's control menu by clicking the control box ▬ to the left of the menu bar, and chose <u>C</u>lose.

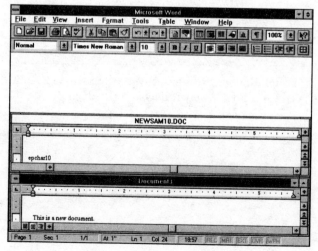

You have closed the extra window on this document.

Make the **NEWSAM10.DOC** *window active by clicking it, and maximise it by clicking* ▲

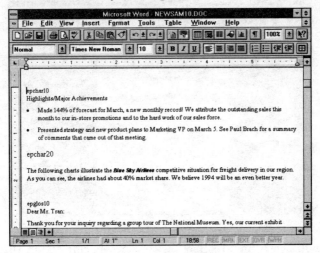

Word can also show the text and pictures of a page in a way that very closely resembles that of the page after it is printed. The facility is known as Print Preview, and in it you can display on the screen the positions of text and pictures exactly. You cannot edit the document during preview, but you can zoom in and out to help you see the way the document will be structured.

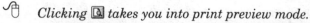

Clicking 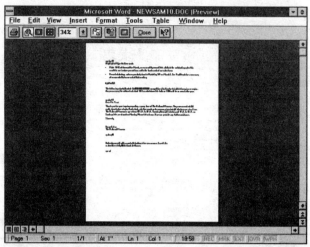 *takes you into print preview mode.*

You will see a new toolbar on the screen, and using this will allow you to see your document in multipage view (▦) or full screen view (▣) by clicking the respective buttons.

If your document covers more than one page, use ▦ to see the flow of the text over the paper.

The preceding screenshot shows a two page print preview from this book during its editing. Clicking ▦ will produce a drop down list from which you can use the left mouse button to select the number of pages you wish to display. The above picture shows 1 row of 2 pages, but many other combinations are available.

Other facilities available from this mode include printing 🖨 if you like what you see, Zoom drop-down list 120% ⬇, help ▶? and Close .

Summary: Views

- The **zoom** list gives access to various magnifications.
- By clicking ▤ you can see the document in **normal** view which is more of a draft view than page layout view.
- ▣ changes the view to **page layout** in which the page is shown as it will be printed.
- You can **split** a window to give separate **panes,** providing two views of the same document.
- You can have different documents in different windows and view them all together by using **Arrange All** from the W̲indow menu.
- You can create two windows for the same document by selecting **N̲ew Window** from the W̲indow menu.

7

PRINTING YOUR DOCUMENT

This chapter covers:
- Using the Print button.
- Using the Print dialog to specify which parts of your document are printed.
- How to cancel a print job.

Once you are happy with the way your document looks on the screen, you will probably want to print it.

☞ *It is wise to save a document just before any print operation as sometimes problems with a printer can cause the computer to halt.*

🖱 *Click*

Using makes Word print the current document in its entirety. The currently selected printer will be used. Any settings (see later) that have already been made will be in effect.

> 🖋 *You can get a list of available printers and select from them by choosing File Print then clicking* [Printer...] *from the Print dialog.*

———— Printing via the print dialog ————

For more control over the print operation than that offered by 🖨, use File Print... to display the Print dialog:

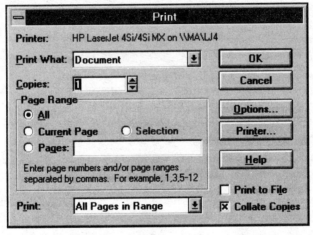

Amongst the controls available here are Copies and Page Range. Here you can set the number of copies to print and choose to print only the Current page, a selected range of pages, or the whole document.

The drop-down list at the bottom of the dialog can be used to arrange to print Odd or Even pages only. This can be useful if you need to produce double-sided copies using a single-side printer. This is done by first printing all the odd pages, and then turning the paper over, feeding it through the printer again and printing the even pages.

[Printer...] displays the Print Setup dialog. Here you will be offered the choice of printers that is available to you (this may be only one; it could even be none if you have no printers set up for use with Windows). You can arrange for subsequent printing to be directed to one of these by selecting the printer (click on its name in the list) and Setting as Default Printer using the button at the bottom of the dialog.

☞ *If you have no printer set up in the Windows Control Panel then Word will not allow access to the printer options such as Print Preview or Print Setup as well as Print.*

Cancelling a print job

From Word

The procedure for cancelling a print operation before Word has completed it depends on whether you have background printing set. You can confirm this by looking at the Print Options dialog (found via Tools Options and using the Print tab).

If background printing is not in use, press Esc to cancel a printing operation whilst the printing dialog is on the screen.

If background printing is in use, choose Print from the File menu, and a special dialog appears where you can stop printing.

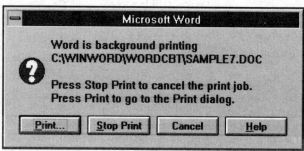

From Print Manager

After leaving Word, the print job will normally pass to the Windows Print Manager. You can switch to the Print Manager using the Task List (pressing ⌷Ctrl⌷⌷Esc⌷). In the Print Manager window, you can identify the printer and select your print job, and then click the Delete button.

From the server

If you are printing to a printer attached to a network and the print job has been forwarded on from Print Manager, you may yet be able to intercept it at the network server. The procedure for this will depend on the network software.

👍 *Once you have cancelled the print job, the printer may still produce printed output. This is because some of the print job has already been sent to the printer and stored in its memory. To prevent the output from appearing you may need to switch the printer off. Be careful when switching off a shared printer as you may also lose other people's work.*

Summary: Printing

- Click 🖨 from the toolbar to print the active document in its entirety to the currently selected printer.
- Choose the <u>P</u>rint... command from the <u>F</u>ile menu to see the options that are available, e.g. number of copies, range of pages, etc.
- You can cancel a print job using a separate Windows program called the **Print Manager** if you have background printing enabled.

8

CLOSING A DOCUMENT

This chapter covers:
- Closing a document that has a filename
- Closing a new document
- Quitting Word

Closing a document that has a filename

🖱 *Switch to the* NEWSAM10 *document.*

👆 *Pull down the File menu and choose Close.*

If you have made changes since this document was last saved, Word will recognise this and ask you if you want to save the latest version now.

It is quite easy to end up with more documents open than you need. You can help avoid this by making a habit of checking the Window menu regularly to ensure you only have required documents open.

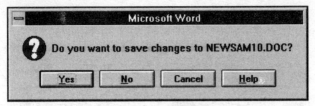

If you get the above dialog, click [Yes] to save your document (and therefore keep changes before closing); or [No] (to close the document without saving changes first).

If you decide you do not want to close the document after all, click [Cancel], and it will be neither saved nor closed.

The NEWSAM10.DOC document is saved with the existing filename and location. If you want to save it with a different filename, or in a different drive or directory, you should use File Save As before closing the document.

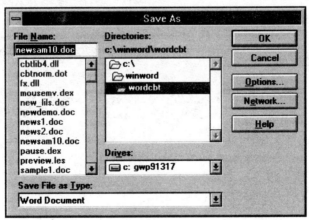

Closing a new document

The new document which you created earlier has not yet been saved as a document, and is labelled Document 3 by Word.

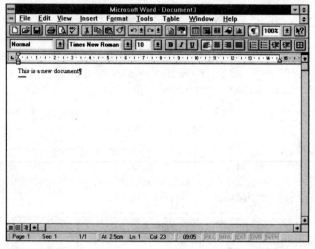

As the document has no name, what will happen if you try to close it?

Use File Close or double-click the document window control menu to close the new document.

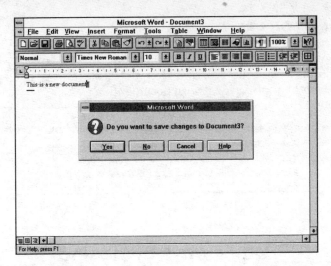

🖱 *Click [**Yes**] on the 'Do you want to Save' dialog.*

This document has no filename, therefore The Save <u>A</u>s dialog is presented. You can specify a filename (and drive and directory if necessary).

🖱 *Name this document* ANOTHER.DOC *(remember you do not have to type the .DOC).*

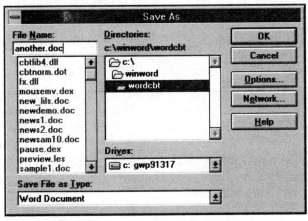

🖱 *Type Another.DOC and close the file. If you have any other documents open, just close them without saving.*

Null menu bar

When you have no documents open, Word displays the Null menu bar. Only the File and Help options are available, since all the other options deal with documents.

 You may be wondering what happened to the document that Word opened for you when you started the application. Since the document was blank and you made no changes to it, Word closed it automatically without presenting the Save As dialog.

_____ Other ways of closing _____
a document

If you have only one window displaying a document, then closing the window will close the document. A window may be closed by clicking the control menu once and choosing Close, or by double-clicking the control menu.

The control menu for the document is obtained by clicking ▣ at the top left of the document window.

If you were to close the whole Word application, any open documents would be closed, and you would be invited to save any unsaved work.

Quitting Windows, by closing the Program Manager, causes all active Windows applications to be closed in an orderly fashion. You would be prompted to save any changes to open Word documents

☝ *If you hold down* [Shift] *while clicking File: the Close option becomes Close All, which can be very useful if you have a number of documents to close at once.*

Quitting Word

When you have finished working with Word, you need to quit the application. This can be done in a number of ways, using the File menu or the application control menu:

- from File choose Exit

- from the application control menu ⊟ choose Close

- double-click the application control menu ⊟. If there is any unsaved work, you will have the usual opportunity to save, giving filenames as necessary.

Summary: Closing and Quitting

- Choose File Close or double-click the document control menu ⊟, to close the active document.
- Use ⌜Shift⌝ with the File menu to obtain the Close All command (to close a number of documents at once).
- Any attempt to close the document, or Word or Windows, before saving any edits will result in a Save Changes? dialog.
- When you quit Word, any open documents are closed, the option to save will be given if changes have been made.

9

SELECTING TEXT

This chapter covers:
- Selecting parts of the document using a mouse and keyboard.
- Deleting text.

In this chapter, you will learn how to select blocks of text of different sizes. This is an important skill in word processing. It is used, for example, in deleting large blocks of text, and also in moving them around within your document. It is also important when you come to change the appearance of your text using formatting – you will have to select the text which you want to format.

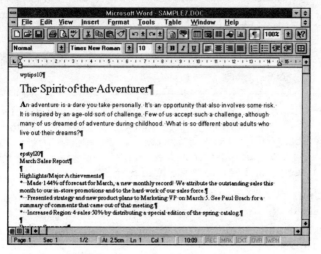

Click 🖱 *and open the document* SAMPLE7.DOC *(in the* WINWORD\EXAMPLES *directory you were using earlier).*

There is a general technique which you should learn before you begin doing useful work.

—— The 'select then do' approach ——

When you make changes to text, the general procedure is always to select what you want to change, and then make the changes: 'select, then do'. On the (hopefully) rare occasions when you cannot remember how to do something, it may help to think 'select, then do'.

> ☞ *Word has a number of special features which it groups under the title 'Intellisense™'. One such feature operates when text formatting is applied and causes Word, by default, to select automatically what it thinks is the right amount of text to be formatted when none has been selected by the user. If you're not sure that the correct text will be selected automatically it does no harm to select it manually instead.*

Once you know how to select the piece of text you require, you are halfway to making important changes to your documents. Remember the procedure is 'select, then do'. When, for instance, a word or part of a document is selected, changes you might decide to make to it include:

- character formatting – making the letters bold, large, coloured
- paragraph formatting – indenting, aligning whole paragraphs
- deleting text
- moving or copying using copy and paste or drag and drop

You will see that 'select, then do' is fundamental to many activities in Word.

> ☞ *Word's default mode of operation is to replace any selected text with any new text that you type. This means that once you have selected text, you should take care not to touch any normal typing key unless you want to replace the selected text. If you do this accidentally and replace text that you wanted to keep, select the Edit menu and the Undo option until the text is restored (you may only need to do this once).*

—— Selecting with the mouse ——

You can select text with a mouse in several ways. The basic technique is to drag the mouse pointer over the text required: the precise behaviour depends on how much text you drag over.

A few letters within a word can be selected by dragging the mouse pointer over them: place the ⊤ at one end of the text to be selected, click and hold down the mouse button, then drag across just a few letters within the same word, releasing the button when the appropriate text is selected. Selected text is shown in reverse colours (usually white letters in a black block).

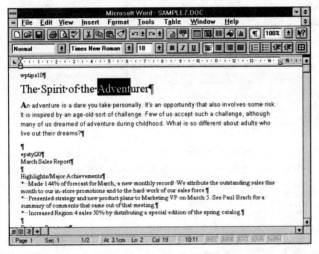

Select **Advent** *in the title of the document, by dragging carefully over part of the word* **Adventurer**.

Word is quite good at 'guessing' what you want to select. For example, when you want to select more than one word by clicking and dragging, the selection is automatically extended to include whole words each time the mouse pointer reaches the beginning of a word. This is designed to prevent you from accidentally selecting only part of a word at the end of a selection where you wanted to select the whole of the last word.

Select the words **dreamed of adventure** *in the first text paragraph, by clicking* **dreamed** *and dragging along the line.*

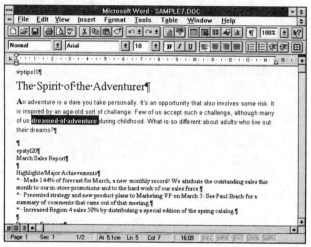

To select one whole word, place the mouse pointer anywhere within the word and double-click. Notice that a following space is usually selected with the word. When formatting a single word, many formatting operations do not require you to select the word: merely placing the insertion point in that word is enough.

You can select in any direction: it does not matter at which end (or corner) of the piece you start. If part of the area you want to select is not shown in the window, simply drag the mouse or cursor off the edge of the window in the relevant direction: the window will scroll.

Selecting a sentence

You could select a sentence by clicking and dragging across all the words in that sentence. However, a quicker method is available. Holding down G while clicking any word in a sentence selects that sentence.

🖑 *Select the entire sentence beginning* **Few of us accept**... *in the second paragraph by positioning the mouse pointer somewhere in the sentence, holding down* ⌨Ctrl *and clicking.*

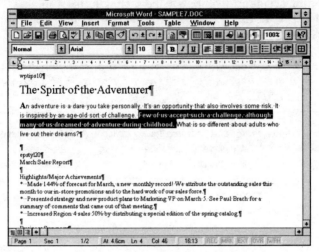

🖑 *Deselect the text by clicking somewhere else in the text or moving the insertion point with the keyboard.*

———— Typing replaces selection ————

Now that you have been selecting portions of text, it is important to emphasise a widely-used Windows feature: that typing replaces selection.

In general in Windows, if a piece of text is selected, whatever is typed next will completely replace it. In Word specifically, it is even possible to replace an entire document in this way! The fact that typing replaces selection can be useful when you are revising a document as you can carefully select only the word(s) you want to replace, then overtype them with as much or as little replacement text as you need (arguably more precise than using the traditional overtype (**OVR**) mode which is toggled on and off using [Insert]).

However, it is easy to do this inadvertently! If you select some text and accidentally press a key, that letter replaces the selected text. If this happens, you can undo it by clicking [↶], pressing [Ctrl][Z] or choosing <u>E</u>dit <u>U</u>ndo (see Chapter 13).

Select the words **live out** *in the first paragraph, and replace them with* **achieve** *without explicitly deleting them first.*

> Look out for places where typing replaces selection can save you time, notably in dialogs where a field entry is selected already when you first open the dialog. For example, in a <u>F</u>ile Save <u>A</u>s dialog, the suggested filename is selected at first so you can immediately type in your preferred filename, rather than wasting time deleting the suggestion.

Selection shortcuts

Whilst dragging is straightforward, selection is such an important technique that Word provides several methods for speeding up the selection of well-defined blocks of text (words, lines, sentences, paragraphs or the whole document). In particular, there is a special area of the document dedicated to the selection process, the **selection bar**. It is the blank area to the left of your text. You can tell when the mouse pointer is in the selection bar because it changes to ↰ when it enters it.

Special selections include:

Word:	Double-click the word (the word includes a space following it, but not any punctuation).
Line:	Click to the left of the line in the selection bar (the mouse pointer is a ⤢ rather than the normal ⤡).
Sentence:	Hold down Ctrl and click within the sentence.
Paragraph:	Double-click in the selection bar to the left of the paragraph.
Multiple words:	Click the first word and, holding down the mouse button, drag through the others.
Multiple paragraphs:	Double-click the selection bar to the left of the first paragraph, and hold down the mouse button on the second click. Then, drag beside the other paragraphs (this is known as double-click and drag.)
Whole document:	Hold down Ctrl and click the selection bar **or** triple-click in the selection bar

   Experiment with selecting different areas of text.

——— Selecting with the keyboard ———

You can select text using the keyboard by placing the flashing insertion point at one end of the text to select, then moving the cursor (using all the available options, e.g. Home and End) while holding Shift.

───── Tips when selecting text ─────

A variant of this last technique involves the mouse and `Shift`. Place the insertion point at the beginning of the text to be selected (for instance by clicking once), hold down `Shift` and use the mouse to click at the end of the text portion. Everything from the first click to the second is selected. This method is useful for selecting large or irregular portions of text.

If you drag with the mouse pointer or move the insertion point downwards or upwards over text using the keyboard, all the text between the starting position and the ending position will be selected. You do not have to cover all the text letter by letter for example, moving one line downwards automatically selects the rest of the line above.

───── Extend selection mode ─────

Repeatedly pressing the **Extend Selection** key `F8` selects, in turn, the current word, line, paragraph and whole document. Once you are using Extend Selection, **EXT** appears darkened on the right of the status bar.

When **EXT** is displayed darkened, typing a character will cause the selection to be extended to that character in your text.

Repeatedly pressing `Shift` `F8` causes the process to work in reverse, selecting smaller bits of text in turn. Pressing `Esc` cancels Extend Selection (**EXT** appears grey in the status bar).

Deleting selected text

Where a large amount of text is to be deleted, it is not convenient to use ⌦ and ⌫ repeatedly. In this case, select the text to be deleted first, then press either ⌫ or ⌦.

Summary: Selection

- To accomplish any task, the technique is always: **select, then do**.
- Selected text is shown as white letters in a black block.
- **Selecting with the mouse**: place the ⊺ at one end of the text, hold down mouse button, then drag across the text. If you drag over more than one word, whole words are selected.
- **Selecting with the keyboard**: position the flashing insertion point at one end of the text, hold down Shift whilst moving with the arrow keys.
- **Selecting a word**: double-click the word.
- **Selecting a line**: using ⇖, click to the left of the line in the selection area.
- **Selecting a sentence**: hold Ctrl and click the sentence.
- **Selecting a paragraph**: double-click the selection area next to the paragraph.
- **Selecting multiple paragraphs**: double-click and drag in the selection area next to the paragraphs.
- **Selecting the entire document**: hold Ctrl and click in the selection bar or triple-click in the selection bar.
- F8 is the **Extend Selection** key. Pressing it repeatedly selects the current word, line, paragraph and whole document in turn. Shift F8 reverses the process. Esc cancels Extend Selection.

10

— DRAG AND DROP —

This chapter covers:
- Using drag and drop to move a selection from one place to another.
- Using drag and drop to copy a selection from one place to another.

—— Moving by drag and drop ——

For those people who would rather do everything with the mouse, it is easy to rearrange text with drag and drop. The basic method is to select the text to move, then drag a special insertion point into position and release the mouse button to complete the action.

🖱 *Select the word **different** in the last sentence of the first paragraph. Move the mouse pointer over the selected word until you see it change shape, then hold the mouse button down and drag to a position in another sentence.*

When you let go of the mouse button, the word **different** should appear at the position you moved to. With some care this technique can also be used to move larger pieces of text.

🖱 *Hold down* Ctrl *and click the sentence beginning **Few of us accept...** (this should select the whole sentence).*

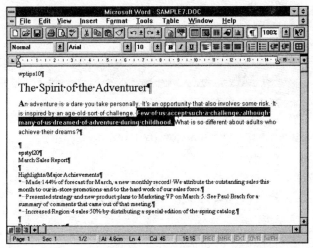

You will move this sentence to the beginning of the paragraph under the heading **Business Summary** (before the word **Our**).

🖱 *Scroll down the screen until you can see the destination paragraph as well as the sentence you are going to move.*

With the sentence selected, position the ⟲ over the selection and hold down the left mouse button. Drag the mouse pointer down towards the new location for the sentence.

Notice that the mouse pointer has changed to ⟲. This is the move pointer. As you drag the move pointer you should see a new striped insertion point (▮) that accompanies the mouse pointer; this is the move cursor.

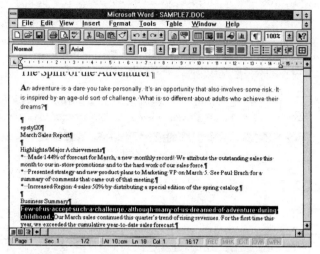

Position the ▮ before the first occurrence of the sentence beginning `Our March sales continued...` and let go of the mouse button.

The sentence has now been moved to the new location.

——— Copying by drag and drop ———

Normally, dragging and dropping causes the selected text to be *moved* from its original place in the document to another. It is also possible to *copy* the text by holding down `Ctrl` when releasing the mouse button.

Try copying the phrase `sort of` *(from the first paragraph) to several positions elsewhere in the text.*

Summary: Drag and drop

- Selected text can be repositioned or copied by drag and drop using the mouse.
- **To move a selection** from one place to another move your mouse cursor over your selection, and drag the selection to the new location.
- **To copy a selection** from one place to another, move your mouse cursor over your selection and hold down `Ctrl` as you drag to the new location.

11

CUT, COPY AND PASTE

This chapter covers:

- Moving information from your document to the windows clipboard.
- Copying information from your document to the windows clipboard.
- Copying (pasting) information from the clipboard back to your document.
- Copying (pasting) information from the clipboard to a different document.
- Using the clipboard to transfer information between different windows applications.

In word processing, and especially in Windows, an important technique for moving pieces of text is cut/copy and paste, as if you were using scissors and glue to rearrange pieces of text on your page. First, the text is cut or copied from the document, then it is pasted back into the document in an appropriate place. Since cut/copy and paste are performed frequently, there are shortcut buttons available on the Standard toolbar, and there are keyboard shortcuts.

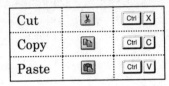

Cut	✂	Ctrl X
Copy	▤	Ctrl C
Paste	▥	Ctrl V

Cutting (or moving)

🖰 *Make sure that paragraph marks are showing (by clicking* ¶ *if necessary).*

Select the paragraph under the heading **The Spirit of the Adventurer.**

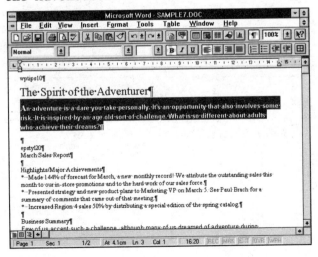

Click

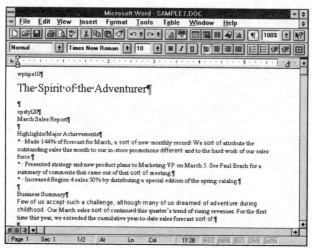

The text disappears, but it has not been lost forever; it is held in an area called the **Clipboard.** The Clipboard is maintained by Windows, and data on the Clipboard will stay there until you cut or copy something else, or exit Windows completely.

> Note that the Clipboard contents can be saved for future sessions by activating the Clipboard Viewer application (from the Program Manager), and using *File Save As...* to save it in file format, and *File Open...* when you want to retrieve the file prior to pasting.

 Move the insertion point to the beginning of the line **Based on the increase...** *which is under the heading* **Revised Market Share Projections.**

Pasting the cut text

You will now retrieve the cut paragraph from the Clipboard:

With the insertion point at the location where the text should be placed, click 🖻

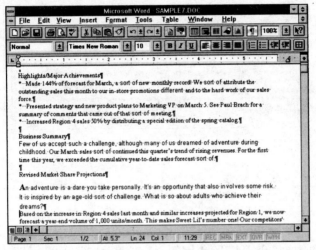

The text that you previously cut has now reappeared at the insertion point. The text still remains in the Clipboard after you have pasted it, so you can paste as many copies as you like.

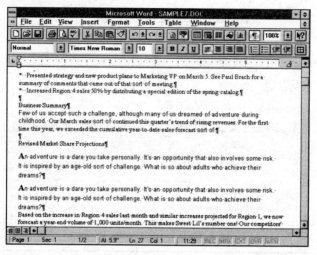

Leaving the insertion point where it is (before the word **Based**), *click* 🔳 *again.*

Copy and paste

Copying text operates in a similar way to cutting, except that the text is not removed from its original location. The text is still placed in the Clipboard and you can still position the insertion point, and paste to place it in a new location in the document, but a copy of the text is left behind in its original position.

🖱 *Select the blank line before* **Product Line Changes** *and the entire paragraph that follows.*

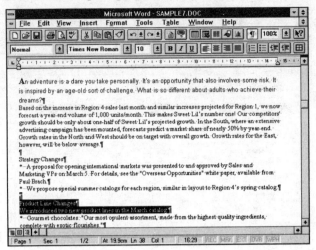

🖱 *Click* 📋 *in the toolbar.*

Position the insertion point on the blank line before the heading **Strategy Changes.**

🖱 *Click* 📋 *in the toolbar.*

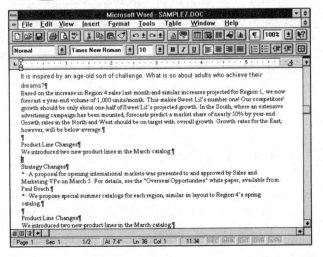

The paragraph has been copied from its original location (and left intact there) and placed in a second, additional location. As with cutting, the Clipboard still contains the copied text and that text can be pasted again as many times as you like (until something else is put in the Clipboard or you exit Windows).

Leaving the insertion point where it is (just before **Strategy Changes**), *click* 🖳 *again.*

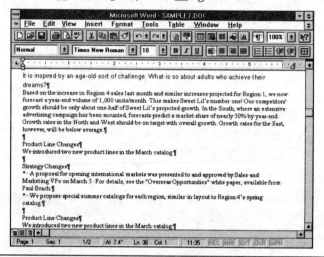

> One advantage of using the ⌷Ctrl⌷ keystrokes is that they function even when you are working in a dialog. This provides a useful way of copying entries into or between fields in a dialog when the *Edit* menu is unavailable.

—— Smart pasting and dragging ——

You may have noticed that when you rearrange words using drag and drop or using cut and paste, Word handles spaces just after the selected text 'intelligently'. Spaces get moved and copied with whole words so as to produce sentences that are properly spaced.

Even if you carefully select only a word without its trailing space and then drag it and drop it within another sentence you will still find it acquires the appropriate number of spaces, and that the text left behind is only left with the right number of spaces.

If you place more spaces than are necessary around a word, then drag the word and drop it into another sentence the spaces will be tidied up automatically.

Experiment with dragging and dropping (and cutting and pasting) words and phrases with and without their spaces.

Exchanging information between documents

One of the important uses of the multiple-document techniques considered earlier is that you can copy or move text from one document to another. For this work you can use either drag and drop (for single copies or moves) or cut/copy and paste (if the same piece of text is likely to be re-used more than once).

To illustrate this, you will produce a new document with certain information extracted from SAMPLE7.DOC, with the minimum of typing.

Without closing SAMPLE7.DOC, use ▣ to create a new document.

Use the Window menu to arrange the two documents horizontally on the screen.

The new document's title can be based on that of the original.

Select the title **The Spirit of the Adventurer** *and drag it into the new document. Do not forget to hold* Ctrl *so as to copy it rather than removing it from the original.*

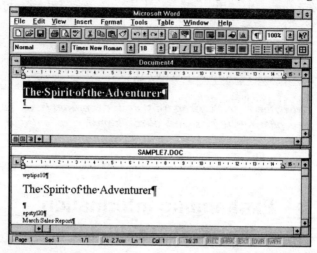

The abbreviated document is to include three paragraphs from SAMPLE7.DOC: the one beginning **An adventure is a dare**; the paragraph headed **Product Line Changes**; and the one headed **Ancient Constellations**.

Now make up the shorter document by dragging and dropping paragraphs (with their headings) between windows. Put in some blank lines to space the work out neatly. Finally maximise the document.

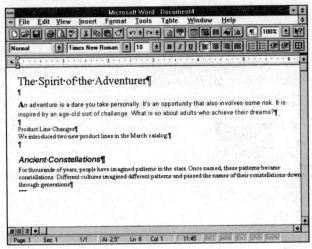

For larger pieces of text you may prefer to use copy and paste, but for short phrases and headings drag and drop can be swifter.

Save the new document, naming it SHORT7

Exchanging information between applications

Cut, copy and paste are techniques that are common to Windows, so you can exchange or copy information between different applications, as well as between documents of the same application.

As a simple example, you will launch Paintbrush, a freehand painting application that comes bundled with Windows 3.1. You will design a logo for your document and copy and paste it onto the SHORT7.DOC. (The general technique works with most Windows applications, e.g. Lotus 1-2-3, Microsoft Project).

🖰 *Launch Paintbrush.*

👍 *You do not need to exit Word: use* `Alt` `Tab` *or* `Ctrl` `Esc` *to switch to the Program Manager and launch Paintbrush from there.*

🖰 *In the Program Manager, find and double-click the icon for Paintbrush. It will probably be in a group called Accessories.*

Use your creative skill and judgement to design an eye-catching logo for the product.

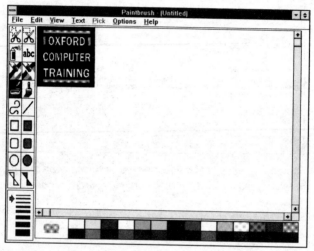

Experiment with choosing a colour by clicking on part of the palette at the bottom of the screen, choosing shape drawing tools and line thicknesses by clicking the icons at the left.

When the logo is ready, select it (click 🔀 and use the cross-hairs and dotted rectangle that appear to enclose your design).

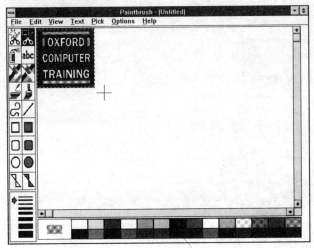

The next part of the procedure should be familiar: having selected the work, look on the Edit menu for a Copy command and use that to copy your logo to the Clipboard.

Choose Edit Copy.

Now you have finished with Paintbrush, you can exit (there is no need to save your work.

Use File Exit or double-click the application control menu in the usual manner.

When you have switched back to the SHORT7 *document, move to the very start of the text (hint:* `Ctrl` `Home`*) and press* `Enter` *twice to insert blank lines. Move the insertion point to the top again.*

Now paste in the logo (use <u>E</u>dit <u>P</u>aste or 🖼 *or* Ctrl V *).*

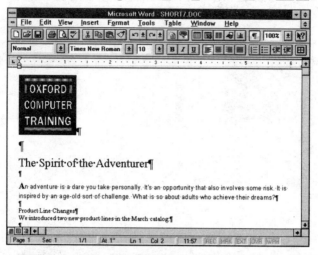

You could paste in a spreadsheet, a graph, or even a sound file that would play when double-clicked into your document using these techniques.

Summary: Cut, copy and paste

- The general technique for **cutting/copying and pasting** is: select the text to be cut/copied; activate cut/copy (by one of the methods below); position the insertion point at the destination and select paste.
- **Activate Cut** by: ✂ or Ctrl X or <u>E</u>dit Cu<u>t</u>.
- **Activate Copy** by: 🖼 or Ctrl C or <u>E</u>dit <u>C</u>opy.
- **Activate Paste** by: 🖼 or Ctrl V or <u>E</u>dit <u>P</u>aste.
- Cut and paste, drag and drop can be used between documents within Word or even between different Windows applications.

12

UNDOING CHANGES

This chapter covers:
- Undoing the last change made to a document.
- Undoing up to the last one hundred changes made to a document.
- Redoing changes that have been undone.

Undoing your last change

At certain times, you will find that the last action you took was a mistake, or didn't work out the way you were expecting. You may decide you want to undo your change. As you work with Word, your actions are recorded. If you want to reverse the effects of these actions, Word will undo the changes made. There are three ways to access Undo: click [▨] on the toolbar, press [Ctrl][Z] or select <u>U</u>ndo from the <u>E</u>dit menu. You will probably find one of these more convenient than the others for your own way of working. What matters is that you remember to use it! You could undo the last paste action if you still have SHORT7.DOC open from the last chapter and have not made any more changes.

Click 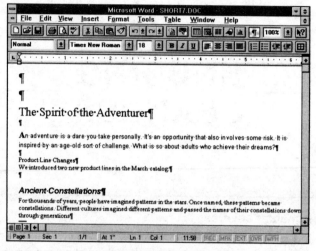 *in the toolbar.*

Notice that the Paintbrush picture has been removed. Note that, if it is still on the Clipboard, you could paste it somewhere different in the document, instead.

There may be occasions when a change cannot be undone. This could be because the change does not affect the document directly (for instance if you modify your toolbars), or because the change is too complicated. Treat undo as a bonus rather than a guaranteed right. Always remember to save your document regularly, particularly if you are making major changes.

──── Undoing several changes ────

Undo in Word can be used repeatedly to undo a succession of changes. It will be more obvious how this operates if you now make a number of edits to your document, then use the undo button several times.

Make several changes to the text, perhaps by using cut/copy and paste, by typing new text, and by deleting text. Then click ⟲ *repeatedly, watching your edits being reversed.*

If you have made several changes before you realise an earlier mistake, you can use undo more selectively.

Display the drop-down list beside the ⟲ *tool.*

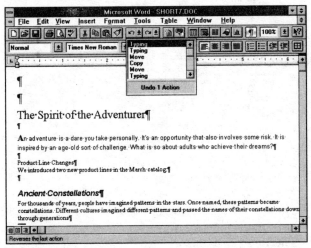

You will recognise the items here as your recent actions. You can now reverse all the changes up to the desired change by selecting from the list. Word will allow you to undo up to the last one hundred changes you have made in your document.

>   You cannot undo just one change from the middle of the list. This could have unpredictable consequences if it is only one of a sequence of actions that have been performed, so Word does not allow it.

Redoing after undo

If you undo once too often make use of on the Standard toolbar. This operates in a similar way to undo, with a drop-down list of recent changes that have just been undone.

Experiment with undoing and redoing changes in your document.

Return the document to a sensible state, then save any changes and close the document.

Summary: Undo

- Undo can reverse up to the last one hundred actions.
- To undo:
    - click ⟲ from the toolbar; or
    - press Ctrl Z; or
    - choose Undo from the Edit menu.
- Undo can be used repeatedly to undo a sequence of recent actions in reverse order.
- A drop-down list of recent actions can be used to undo a selected change, even if other changes have been made since.
- The Redo ⟳ button with drop-down list works in a similar way for redoing changes that should not have been undone.

13

TEXT FORMATTING

This chapter covers:
- Font formatting using the toolbar buttons and menu for bold, italic, underline, font and font size.
- Font formatting using the Font dialog.

So far, you have dealt with everything in the 'normal' or **default** style. A few of the more simple formatting options that are available will now be considered.

Word addresses formatting at four levels in your document:

- **Text formatting:** characters and words
- **Paragraph formatting:** paragraphs
- **Section formatting:** groups of paragraphs
- **Document formatting:** the whole document

For now, you will be concerned only with text and paragraph formatting: these are available on the Format menu. As you will see, several of the most frequently used text and paragraph formatting options are also available from the Formatting toolbar. This toolbar is doubly useful since it displays the formats that have been applied to the text in which the insertion point is currently located (or the selected text) as well as allowing you to change formatting.

☞ *You can also use* ⯆? *to tell you what formats have been applied to a particular piece of text. Use* ⌜Esc⌟ *to end the help.*

The formatting toolbar

You have already seen that ⟦B⟧, ⟦I⟧ and ⟦U⟧ can be used to apply or remove formatting. They can also be used as indicators of whether the formatting has been applied to text, based on the way the button is displayed: 'depressed' or released.

Let's suppose that you would like to go through the document and make some of the headings bold and underlined.

🖑 *Click the selection bar to the left of the* **Highlights/Major Achievements** *heading to select it.*

🖑 *Click* ⟦B⟧ *and* ⟦U⟧ *on the Formatting toolbar. Click somewhere else on the page to remove the selection so you can see the effects of your action.*

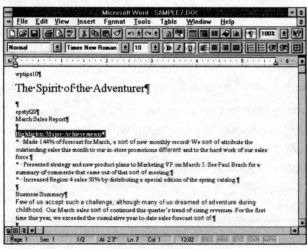

Click to place the insertion point in the formatted text. Notice how the buttons appear to depress, to show the options applied to the current text. This is an important feature of Word buttons because it allows you to 'see' which formats have been applied to the selected bit of text.

Now continue down the document, making the next four headings bold and underlined. Remember to <u>select</u> the heading (by clicking in the selection bar to its left), then click **B** *to <u>do</u> the operation.*

The next four headings are:

- **Business Summary**
- **Revised Market Share Projections**
- **Product Line Changes**
- **Strategy Changes**

I works in the same way as **B**, applying or removing italic format to the selected text.

Press Ctrl Home *to move to the top of the document. Double-click the word* **Spirit** *in the title* **The Spirit of the Adventurer**. *Click* **I** *in the toolbar.*

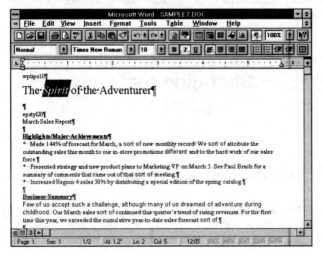

The selected text is now italicised and 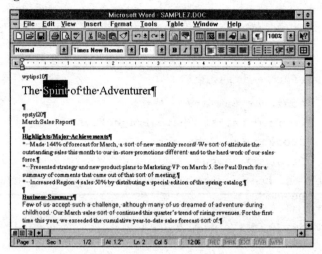 is shown depressed. Now assume that this text should not be italicised after all. So how do you remove italic for this text (apart, of course, from using Undo)?

*With the same text selected (re-select it if necessary), click *
again.

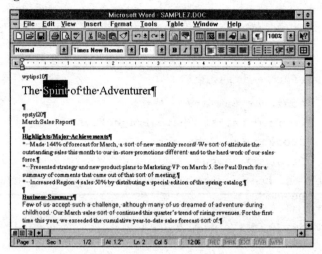

Notice that the text is now 'normal' again and is in its 'off' or non-depressed position.

Changing fonts and point sizes

Pull down lists for the font and point size

If you want to change the font of a heading in the document, you can use the pull-down fonts list on the Formatting toolbar.

🖱 *Press* ⌈Ctrl⌉ ⌈Home⌉ *to move to the top of the document, then select the* **Highlights/Major Achievements** *heading by clicking in the selection bar to its left.*

🖱 *Pull down the list of available fonts by clicking* ⊡ *to the right of the font box on the Formatting toolbar.*

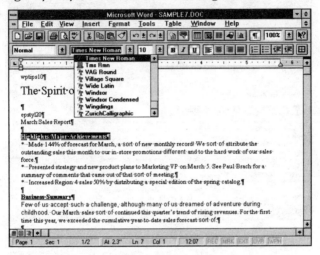

🖱 *Select the 'Arial' font from the list by clicking it (you may need to scroll upwards to find 'Arial').*

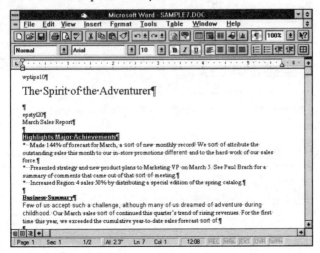

The font of the selected text has now changed to Arial.

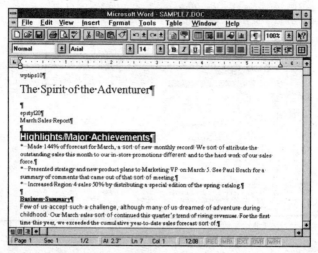

Pull down the list of available font sizes. Change the point size to 14 by clicking 14 in the list.

(Note: there are 72 points to the inch.)

Continue down the document, changing the font and point size for the next four headings (change the font to 'Arial' and the point size to 14).

In general, if you have a large number of headings to format you would use a style – these will be discussed later. For the moment, this is good practice for 'select, then do'.

All the headings are now formatted and stand out nicely in the document.

An aside about fonts

You may be wondering about the different symbols next to the font names on the font menu. The meanings of the symbols are shown in the table below:

T̅r	TrueType fonts. These look the same on screen as when printed. They are known as 'scaleable' fonts, which means they are available in a wide variety of point sizes. As such they will often be the favourite choice.
🖳	Printer fonts. These fonts are available based on the current printer. Being dependent on the type of printer makes these fonts less versatile, but they will usually print very quickly. The closest matching screen font will be used to approximate the selected printer font on the screen.
(blank)	Windows screen fonts. These are used to display data on screen. these fonts *may* print satisfactorily but the closest matching font in the printer will be used, so results can be unpredictable.

> *It is possible to display TrueType fonts only. In Program Manager, choose Fonts from the Control Panel, click TrueType... and check* ☒ *Show Only TrueType Fonts in Applications.*

Text formatting using the dialog

The Font dialog shows the current character formats applied to the selected text, as does the Formatting toolbar.

The basic idea is to select the characters you want to format, activate the Font dialog, set the new attributes of the text and then click ▭ OK ▭. The attributes are set by checking or unchecking boxes, making selections from pull-down lists or entering values for spacing and the like. You can activate this dialog by choosing F̲ont from the Fo̲rmat menu or by right-clicking the selected text and choosing Font... from the shortcut menu.

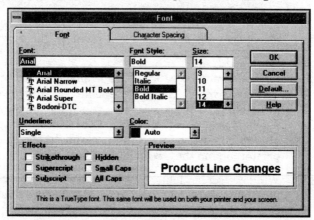

    Select the **Product Line Changes** *heading (if it is not al-
ready selected) and then call up the Font dialog.*

This is one of Word's **tabbed dialogs** – it is divided into two parts and you can switch between them by clicking the tabs ('Fo̲nt' or 'Cha̲racter Spacing') near the top. We will assume that you are presented with the Fo̲nt tab first: Word remembers the last tab used so you may be presented with either on activating the dialog. 'Cha̲racter Spacing' will be covered shortly.

Notice the Preview area. Changes you make in this dialog will be reflected on a mock-up in the Preview area so that you can see what the text will look like without leaving the dialog. Preview areas are common in Word dialogs.

Pull down lists for C̲olor and U̲nderline style are available here (these are not available from the default Formatting toolbar – the toolbar underline always gives single line style). You can also choose a F̲ont Style and S̲ize, either by selecting from the list or by typing the value you require in the edit box.

Notice also that there are additional attributes for 'Style' (Stri̲kethrough, Hi̲dden, S̲mall Caps and A̲ll Caps). The Superscript and Subscript styles make the selected text smaller as well as changing the position of the text on the line.

Try some of these options, keeping an eye on the Preview area. Click the Character Spacing tab to switch to the other half of this Font dialog.

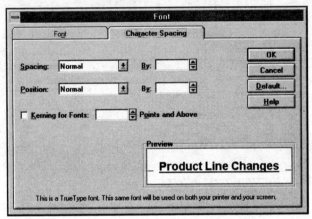

You can vary the spacing (horizontal, or distance between characters) and position (vertical, or offset from the line) of the text.

The 'By' boxes allow you to control how far characters are spaced. The tiny up and down arrow buttons ⬍ (known as spinners) allow you to increase or decrease a value in the attached text box.

Experiment with these options in the current document.

Kerning is the term used in typesetting for the adjustment of spacing between certain combinations of characters, such as the 'WA' combination, where the spacing between them is altered for a neater effect. In the case of 'WA' the two letters would be moved closer together. With small fonts, the effect is often negligible (and just wastes computer time in calculating) so Word allows you to switch on Kerning above a certain specified size. This allows you, for example, to choose to use kerning for headings, but not paragraph text.

——— Capitalisation/uppercase ———

The Font dialog offers formats for S_m_all Caps and A_ll Caps, simply altering the look of the characters. An alternative method is to use F_o_rmat Change Cas_e_... . The quickest way to show how Change Cas_e_... works is through an example.

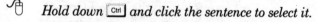 *Move to the end of the document by pressing* `Ctrl` `End` *and then press* `Enter` *a few times to create some blank lines.*

Type the following sentence on the last line of the document (note the uppercase letters):

Now is the time for all Good People to come to the aid of THE country.

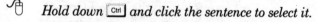 *Hold down* `Ctrl` *and click the sentence to select it.*

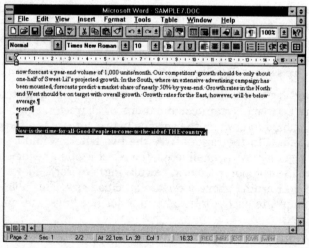

🖰 *Choose For̲mat Change Cas̲e... and pick ⦿ T̲itle case.*

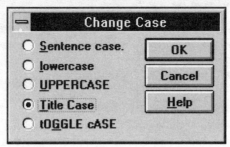

🖰 *Now click* [OK]

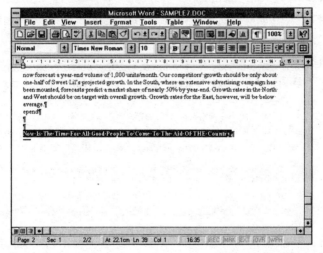

Note that the entire sentence has been changed to 'Title case', which means that the initial letter of each word has been capitalised (note that this does not affect any other characters – 'THE' is still entirely capitalised).

🖰 *Try some of the other options on For̲mat Change Cas̲e... and experiment with the shortcut key* Shift F3*, which can be used to cycle through the first 3 options in the For̲mat Change Cas̲e... dialog: sentence case, lowercase and uppercase. The first usage of* Shift F3 *reformats the selected text according to one of these cases, the choice being dependent on the formatting of the text when it was selected. Subsequent uses of*

[Shift] [F3] *on that same text will cycle through the other two options and then back to the first.*

You may have noticed that once you've used [Shift] [F3] *if the text was not
originally formatted in sentence case, lower case or upper case, it
never returns to its original form. However, you could revert the text to
its original format using the Undo facility.*

If necessary, click Undo [↶ ▾] *until the text reverts to its original state.*

Summary: Font formatting

- The basic appearance of a character is affected by its
  font and its point size available in pull down lists from
  the Formatting toolbar.
- Characters may be formatted using attributes such as
  Bold, *Italic* and <u>Underline</u>. Buttons for each of these
  appear on the Formatting toolbar.
- The format of existing characters can be changed by
  selecting the text and then choosing the appropriate
  buttons or lists in the Formatting toolbar to do the operation.
- The buttons on the Formatting toolbar are shortcuts for
  some of the most commonly-used font formats. Access-
  ing all the font formats at once requires the Format
  Font dialog.
- The Format Font dialog can be accessed by choosing
  Font... from the Format menu or by right-clicking selected text and choosing Font... from the shortcut
  menu.

14

PARAGRAPH FORMATTING

This chapter covers:

- Paragraph formatting using the toolbar.
- Indents and alignment.
- Paragraph formatting using the paragraph dialog.

Word defines a paragraph as a piece of text ending with a paragraph marker ¶ (a paragraph marker, which by itself can also be considered a paragraph!). Word offers a number of formatting options which can be applied to a whole paragraph.

—— Indenting using the toolbar ——

Add indent button

Sometimes, you will want a block of text to be indented from the normal left margin. This can be done quickly using the Add Indent button (🔢)

🖐 *Scroll down to the heading **Highlights/Major Achievements** at the end of the document and select the first paragraph beneath it by clicking to its left in the selection bar.*

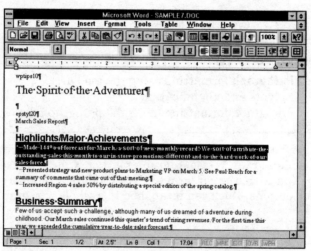

Click 🖶 on the Formatting toolbar.

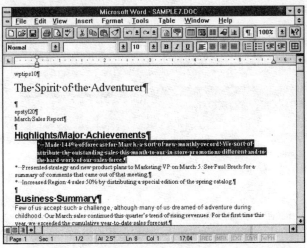

Notice that the line has been indented 0.5" from the left margin (evident from the 🖺 markers on the ruler and from the position of the text on the screen). Looking at the result, you may decide that 0.5" is not enough and 1" would be better:

Click 🖶 again.

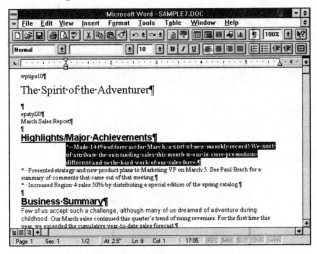

The line has been indented a further 0.5".

It would be a bit tedious to indent each paragraph you wanted indented in this fashion; there is an easier way:

Select the next two paragraphs by clicking in the selection bar to the left of the first line you want and dragging down until the remaining lines are selected.

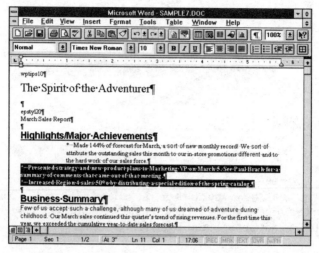

Click ⊞ *twice to indent the selected paragraphs 1" (the same as the first paragraph).*

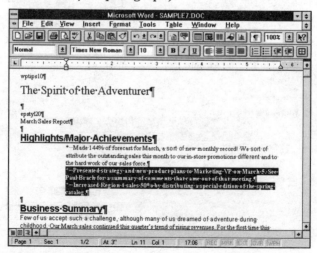

The entire paragraph is now indented 1". However, after seeing it indented 1" you may still not be satisfied that it's right. You can indent it a further 0.5" to see if that's any better.

Use the selection bar to select the entire section that you have indented, then click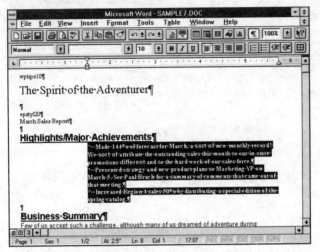

Maybe you're not happy with this 1.5" indent at all and now you're sure that it looked better before. The solution is to re-move an indent (or 'un-indent') using ▦.

Remove indent button

With the entire section still selected (select it again if nec-essary), click ▦ *on the Formatting toolbar.*

The text is now back to its 1" indent.

The method of indenting

When word processing (as against using a typewriter), you should never use spaces to indent a line, since this does not allow you to adjust all indents automatically. Also, if you had used spaces and then changed the font of the paragraph, the size of the spaces would change, and hence the size of the indent. When using a proportionally-spaced font it can be very difficult to line up work that has been 'indented' using many spaces.

Indenting using the ruler

From the ruler it is possible to control formatting for three types of paragraph indents: left or body text indent (which you have just been dealing with), right indent or temporary right margin (where the position of the right edge of a paragraph is altered), and first line indent (where only the position of the first line is altered). These three factors can be set independently. For example: the first line of a paragraph may be indented to 1.5" while the main body can be indented 1" from the left margin and 2" from the right margin.

As the indent for the first line of a paragraph can be set separately, it is also possible for this first line to be given a smaller indent, to produce a 'hanging indent':

> This is the first line of the paragraph: indented to 0.5",
> while this is the second line, indented to 1". If
> you add further lines, you can see the effect of
> the main body indent.

The ruler shows what the states of both these factors are. Near the left side of the ruler are two triangles and a rectangle marker: ⌂

- the position of the first line indent is shown by the upper (downward-pointing) triangle

- the position of the main body indent is shown by the lower (upward-pointing) triangle.

Remember, this is a per-paragraph setting; should you want to make the whole document narrower, you could change the page margins in the Page Setup dialog (to be covered later in this book).

You can set the indents for a paragraph (or selected group of paragraphs) by dragging any of these markers along the ruler.

Select the last but one paragraph (beginning **Based on the increase in Region 3...**) *and change the indent of the first line only by dragging the upper triangle at the left of the Ruler to 2".*

Now change the left indent of the body of the paragraph by dragging the lower triangle at the left of the ruler to 1".

Note that altering the indentation of the body in this way does not alter the indentation of the first line.

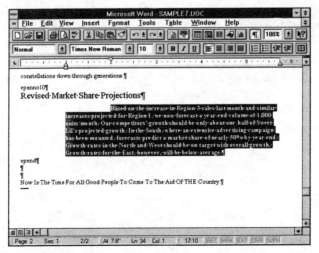

Just below the lower triangle on the ruler you should see a grey rectangle. Dragging this moves both left-hand indent markers together, while maintaining their relative positions.

🖰 *Move both indent markers together by dragging the rectangle marker to 2".*

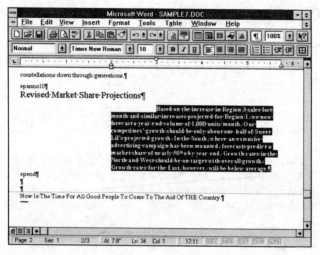

🖰 *Scroll up to find the heading* **The Orchestra**. *Double-click and drag in the selection bar to select both of the paragraphs under this heading. Notice how the first line indent also moves.*

🖰 *Set the first line indent of the selection to 0.5" on the ruler. (Make sure that you only drag the first line indent marker, and leave the main body indent marker at 0".)*

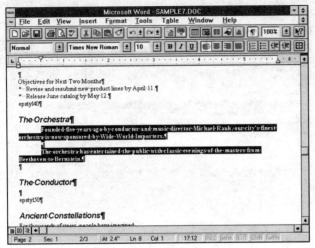

Notice that both paragraphs have been indented in the same manner and by the same distance.

🖰 *Drag the main (square) indent marker to 0.5" and drag the first line indent back to 0" to make hanging indents on the selected paragraphs*

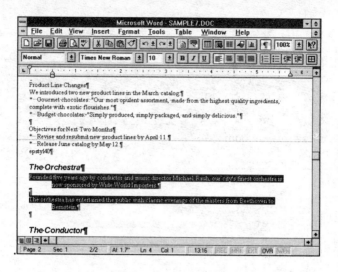

Product Line Changes¶
We introduced two new product lines in the March catalog.¶
* Gourmet chocolates: "Our most opulent assortment, made from the highest quality ingredients, complete with exotic flourishes."¶
* Budget chocolates: "Simply produced, simply packaged, and simply delicious."¶
¶
Objectives for Next Two Months¶
* Revise and resubmit new product lines by April 11.¶
* Release June catalog by May 12.¶
epstyl40¶

The Orchestra¶

Founded five years ago by conductor and music director Michael Rauh, our city's finest orchestra is now sponsored by Wide World Importers.¶
¶
The orchestra has entertained the public with classic evenings of the masters from Beethoven to Bernstein.¶
¶

The Conductor¶

Keystrokes for indenting paragraphs

The following keyboard equivalents are available for indenting quickly:

`Ctrl` `M`	increases main and first line indents by the default tab stop setting (which can be changed in Format, Paragraph, Tabs...)
`Ctrl` `Shift` `M`	decreases main and first line indents by the default tab stop setting
`Ctrl` `T`	increases hanging indent (i.e. that of the body text) to the nearest default tab stop
`Ctrl` `Shift` `T`	decreases hanging indent (i.e. that of the body text) to the nearest default tab stop

 Leaving the paragraphs selected, try out some of the keyboard equivalents for indenting (listed above) on other paragraphs of the document.

Aligning text

We have experimented with the indentation of text but until now all our text has been left-aligned or 'left-justified', i.e. the first word of each line has been aligned with the left edge of the page. Word also allows text to be centre- or right-aligned.

Word alignment is a feature of a whole paragraph. An alignment setting cannot be applied to just part of a paragraph: it would be meaningless to attempt to centre one word within a paragraph.

You are going to centre a title, but first of all let's apply some font formats for revision:

🖰 *Select the title* `The Spirit of the Adventurer` *(click to its left in the selection bar). Click* **B***, then* **U***, then change the font to Arial and the point size to 16 using the appropriate pull down lists.*

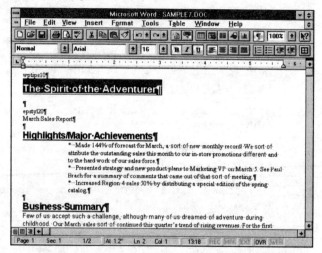

Paragraph alignment using toolbar buttons

The title is now the size and shape we want but it might look better on a different place on the page. Notice that the Left Alignment button ▤ in the Formatting toolbar is depressed. This means that left alignment is currently applied to the selected title paragraph. Let's try some other alignments.

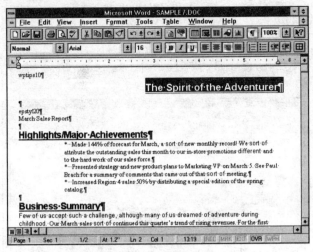

With the title selected, click the Right Alignment button
⊞ *– (you may want to scroll or reduce the zoom size of your document to see the result of this).*

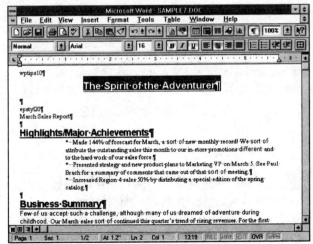

With the title selected, click ⊞.

The title is centred between the margins.

Word allows for fully-justified alignment, but this is more sensibly applied to longer paragraphs: ⊞ increases the space between the words so that both the left and right margins of the paragraph are straight (as in this paragraph you are reading). However, the last line of the paragraph remains left aligned and no space is added; it might look odd to stretch out a line that has for example only four words.

Select the three paragraphs under the heading **High-lights/Major Achievements** *and click* 🔲 *to justify them.*

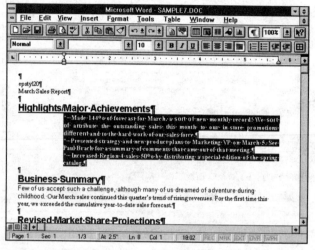

Notice how the body of the paragraph is justified while the last line is not.

Paragraph formatting using the dialog

As with character formats, there are other options for paragraph formatting that do not appear on the Formatting toolbar or the ruler. These are available in the Paragraph dialog from the Format menu. This is another tabbed dialog, divided between Indents and Spacing and Text Flow. The Indents and

Spacing tab is relevant to the work you have just done; aspects of Text Flow will be considered later in the book.

You can bring up this dialog by selecting Format Paragraph... or by right-clicking in the paragraph to be changed then choosing Paragraph from the shortcut menu.

Leave the three paragraphs selected (or select them again if necessary) and then use the Format menu to bring up the Paragraph dialog.

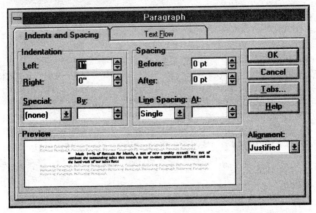

Notice immediately that this dialog also has a Preview area.

Controls under Spacing allow you to set the format for a paragraph to include blank lines both Before and After the paragraph and to set the paragraph's Line Spacing (single, one-and-a-half, double, etc.). These Spacing options are a much better (i.e. 'softer') way of creating blank space before, within and after paragraphs, rather than typing blank lines by pressing Enter.

> Since line spacing options are formats, they become very important with respect to styles. See the later chapter on styles for more information.

The Alignment pull down list reflects the current setting of the alignment buttons in the Formatting toolbar and allows you to change them. Indentation controls reflect the current settings of the indent markers in the ruler and can also be changed explicitly (this can be more accurate than dragging on the ruler).

`Tabs...` (below `Cancel`) will accept any changes made to the Paragraph dialog and then bring up the Tabs dialog. The Text Flow options and the Format Tabs dialog are also accessed through Format Tabs...

Using the selected paragraphs, experiment with paragraph spacing, alignment and indentation using the Paragraph dialog.

You may have discovered that when paragraph formatting a single paragraph it isn't necessary to select it all. It is enough for the insertion point to be in the paragraph so that Word knows which paragraph to format. When formatting more than one paragraph it is enough to select at least one character of each paragraph again so Word knows which paragraphs to include.

To reset some of the paragraphs you have been experimenting with to something more normal: select the paragraphs and press `Ctrl` `Q` to reset their paragraph formatting to the default for the document template.

Summary: Paragraph formatting

- The ⊞ button adds indents to selected paragraphs.
- The ⊞ button removes indents from selected paragraphs.
- Paragraph indenting is controlled by three factors: the first line indent, the main text (or body) indent and the right indent. These appear on the ruler as triangle markers ⧍ and ⧌. Moving one of the markers on the ruler adjusts the format of the selected paragraph(s) accordingly. The rectangle which appears under the main text indent marker can be used to move main text and first line indent in parallel.
- There are four buttons in the Formatting toolbar that control paragraph alignment:
    - ▤ adds or removes left alignment
    - ▤ adds or removes centre alignment
    - ▤ adds or removes right alignment
    - ▤ adds or removes justified alignment
- Certain frequently-used paragraph formatting options can be accessed from the Formatting toolbar and the ruler – options also available from the paragraph dialog (via the Format menu).
- The Format Paragraph dialog can be accessed by choosing Paragraph... from the Format menu (or the short cut menu) or by double-clicking in the upper half of the ruler.
- Ctrl Q resets the formatting of the selected paragraphs.

15

BULLETED AND NUMBERED LISTS

This chapter covers:

- Applying bullets and numbered lists using the toolbar.
- Removing bullets and numbered lists.

There are times when a bulleted or numbered list is an appropriate way of presenting items or points in a document. Word can generate such lists through the use of ▤ and ▤.

—————— Bullets button ——————

An example of a bulleted list looks something like this:

- point 1
- point 2
- point 3
- etc.

The procedure for creating bulleted lists in Word is quite simple and follows the 'select, then do' approach. First, select the paragraphs that you want bulleted, then click the ⊞ button in the Standard toolbar to add a bullet before each.

As with alignment and indent formatting in the previous chapter, bulletting is a feature that is applied to a whole paragraph. So if you want to set up a bullet symbol and indent on just one paragraph you do not have to select the whole paragraph, just click anywhere in the paragraph and then use ⊞.

To experiment with bullets and numbering, you will open a new document from the WORDCBT directory.

Open the file C:\WINWORD6\WORDCBT\SAMPLE1.DOC

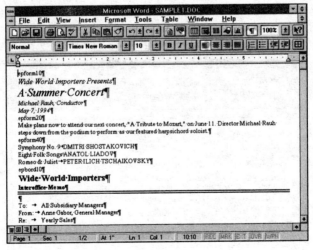

Select or click in the single line under the heading **A Summer Concert** and then click ▤

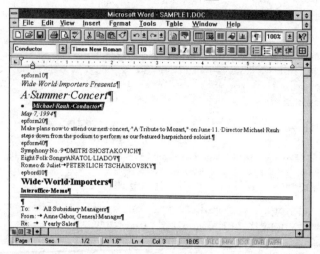

The main body of the paragraph has now been indented 0.25" and it has a bullet as its first character.

Repeat this for the line: **May 7th, 1994.**

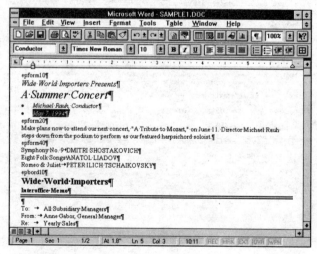

To see more clearly the effect that inserting a bullet point has on the paragraph format of text, add a bullet point to a longer paragraph:

*Click somewhere in the paragraph starting **Make plans now...** and then insert a bullet point.*

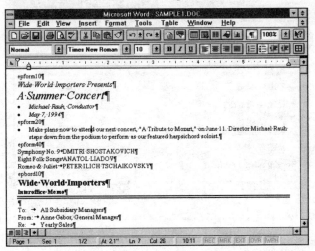

Not only is the first line indented, but subsequent lines are also indented. The paragraph now has a hanging indent (which you looked at earlier), the bullet symbol is part of the first line. You can verify this by choosing Format Paragraph whilst the insertion point is still in the paragraph.

It is not necessary to apply bullet points to paragraphs one at a time: they can be applied to a block of lines using the select, then do principle. Assume that you have decided to emphasise the paragraph entitled 'Precious Stones' using bullets and extra line spacing.

*Scroll down to the heading **Precious Stones**. At the end of the first line under this heading (**Diamonds**) press* Enter. *Do the same at the end of the next line.*

*Highlight the lines from **Diamonds** through to **Emerald**.*

Effectively you have selected five paragraphs.

Press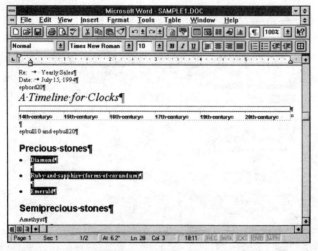

Notice that bullet points have been applied only to those paragraphs with text: empty paragraphs have not had bullet points added.

—————— Numbered list button ——————

Numbered lists are similar to bulleted lists, but with the bullet symbols replaced with sequential numbers.

 Under the `Semiprecious stones` *heading, select the list of stones (from* `Amethyst` *to* `Opal`*).*

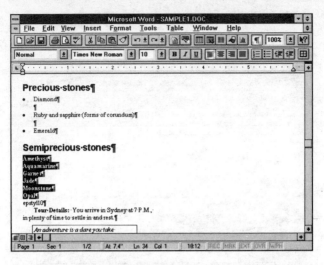

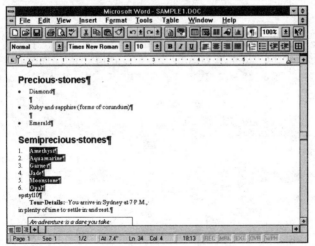

Click ☰ on the Formatting toolbar.

The points have been indented 0.25" and have been numbered sequentially.

If you want a series of paragraphs to be numbered in sequence, you need to select all the relevant paragraphs and number them in one action.

Scroll up to the heading **A Summer Concert** *and highlight the list of three pieces of music under it.*

Click 🔲

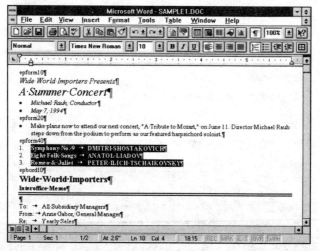

These numbers are to a certain extent automatic: if you rearrange numbered paragraphs by dragging and dropping or by inserting new paragraphs, the numbers maintain the current order.

 Demonstrate this by dragging the second paragraph after the third.

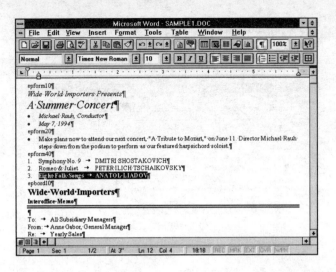

—— Removing bullets or numbers ——

The procedure for removing bullets or numbers is, as you might expect, to click in or select the paragraph in question then release the 🔢 or 🔢 button (notice that these buttons will be shown depressed when the current paragraph has the relevant format).

 Remove the bullet from the paragraphs under the heading **Precious Stones***.*

A special case arises when a sequence of paragraphs has been numbered and you try to remove numbering from just one of those paragraphs.

Try this: click in the paragraph numbered 2 under the heading A Summer Concert *and click* 📋

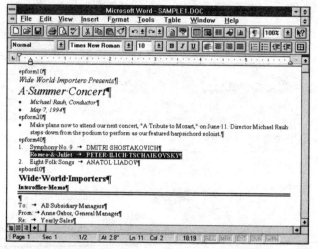

What happens? The number certainly disappears, but look closely. The paragraph has not returned to its previous indent, and the paragraph following it has been renumbered. In fact you have not removed the numbering format from this paragraph, merely skipped numbering. Skip numbering is available on the shortcut menu.

If you really need to remove the numbering format from a single paragraph (and return it to its original indent) right-click the paragraph and use Stop Numbering from the shortcut menu.

You may like to investigate the F̲ormat Bullets and N̲umbering... dialog, where you will find much more control over bullets and numbering. This dialog is also available from the shortcut menu.

Click ▣ in the toolbar to save the document under its current name.

Print the document by clicking ▣

Close the document by choosing C̲lose from the F̲ile menu.

Summary: Bullet and number lists

- To make bulleted lists: select the paragraphs to be bulleted, then click ▦
- To make numbered lists: select the paragraphs to be numbered, then click ▦
- The number sequence is maintained automatically if the numbered paragraphs are rearranged.
- Once bulleting or numbering has been applied to a list, further formatting can be applied.
- Bullets can be removed from a paragraph by releasing the ▦ button.
- Numbers can be removed from a whole sequence of paragraphs in a similar way, provided that more than one paragraph is selected.
- If the ▦ tool is released while only one of the numbered paragraphs is selected, that paragraph skips the number but numbering format is not fully removed.

16

PAGINATION CONTROL

This chapter covers:

- Page breaks and page break (pagination) control.

 Open the file C:\WINWORD\WORDCBT\SAMPLE6.DOC *using the Open button on the Standard toolbar.*

Make sure the ruler is displayed. If it isn't, display it by selecting <u>R</u>uler from the <u>V</u>iew menu.

 *SAMPLE6.DOC has been set up to allow you to create an automatic table of contents and index. To do this it inserts **field codes** after each heading. Using the <u>T</u>ools <u>O</u>ptions... dialog. Word has been told not to show you these codes, and only to show the paragraph markers. This is not something you would normally need to do when editing a document (unless, of course, you had previously switched these on).*

🖰 *Choose Tools Options... and select the View tab. In the Nonprinting Characters frame, make sure that only ☒ Paragraph Marks is selected.*

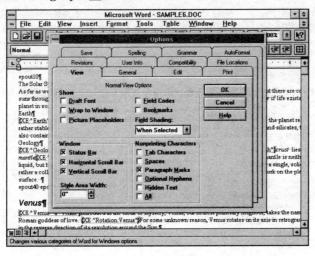

🖰 *Click*

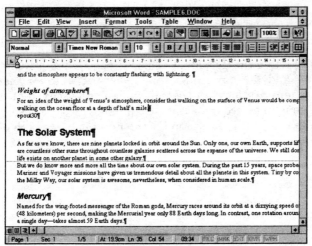

🖰 *Use the scroll bars to view the document.*

Note that there are some page breaks (dotted lines across the screen) in places that will make the document difficult to read when it is printed, such as in the middle of paragraphs. These page breaks are put in automatically by Word and take account of how much material of any kind it considers makes the best fit for a page. This does not always produce a satisfactory result, as you can see below.

Move to the bottom of page 2 so you can see the `Green-house effect` *heading.*

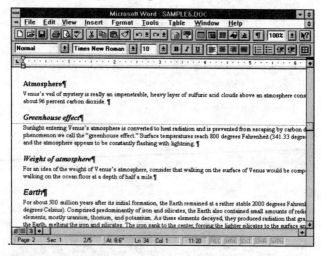

It would make the document easier to read when printed if the heading and the paragraph that follows it were on the same page. There are formats that allow you to specify that a page break must not occur in certain circumstances. These can be found in the Text Flow section of the Format Paragraph dialog.

Select the paragraph `Greenhouse effect`*, then choose the* <u>P</u>*aragraph option from the* F<u>o</u>*rmat menu. Select the Text* <u>F</u>*low tab in the dialog.*

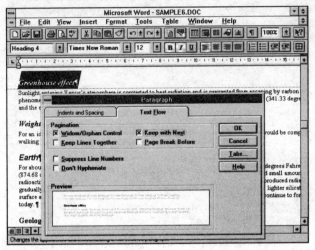

Keep with next

This heading has been separated from the body paragraph to which it refers by a 'soft' page break, one that Word has inserted itself and one that will move if the amount of text earlier in the document has changed. Word allows you to tie paragraphs together so that the page will not break between them:

🖰 *In the Format Paragraph dialog, check ☒ Keep with Next.*

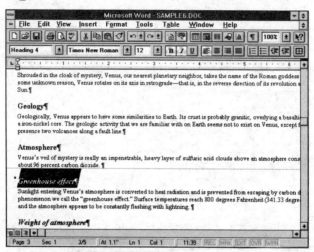

The page break between this heading and its paragraph moves above the heading. The heading paragraph may be thought of as being 'connected' to the paragraph that follows, and no page break is allowed to separate them.

🖰 *Scroll down to the bottom of the document. Type in the following text:*

The Solar System is made up of: `Enter` `Enter`
The `Sun` `Enter`
Mercury `Enter`
Venus `Enter`
Earth `Enter`
Mars `Enter`
Asteroids `Enter`
Jupiter `Enter`
Saturn `Enter`
Uranus `Enter`
Neptune `Enter`
Pluto `Enter`

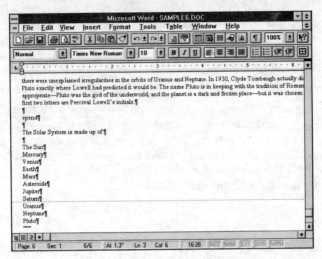

Suppose you want to prevent these paragraphs from being split by a page break and thus keep the list together on one page. How could you accomplish this? The answer is to:

Select **The Solar System is made up of** *to Neptune and check* ⊠ *Keep With Ne*x*t in the F*o*rmat P*a*ragraph dialog. Click* [OK]

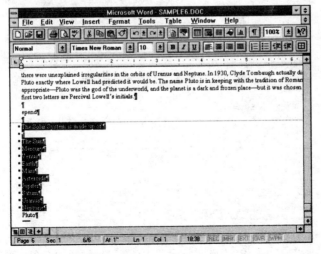

In order to keep these paragraphs together, you formatted all but the last paragraph as 'Keep With Next': the first will be linked to the second, which will be linked to the third, which will be linked to the fourth, and so on.

It is important to be clear about why you did not format all the lines as keep with next. Remember that you are marking each selected paragraph to stay with the <u>next</u> paragraph. If you had done that to the last paragraph (and had there been any paragraphs after that) this last paragraph would have been linked to the next, which would probably have been unnecessary, and possibly confusing later on.

Page break before

Move to the top of the document and then scroll down until you can see both the page break between pages 1 and 2 and the heading `The Solar System`.

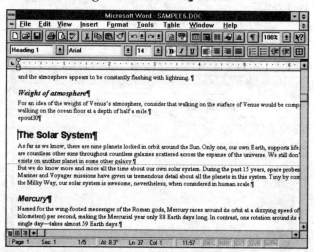

Suppose you would like this major heading `The Solar System` to start at the top of a new page, so as to emphasise the topic. You can use the <u>P</u>age Break Before option to achieve this.

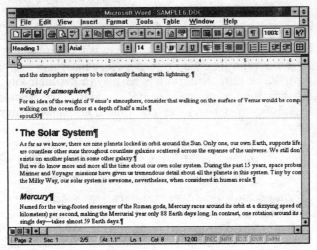

Place the insertion point in the heading **The Solar System** *From the Format Paragraph dialog, check* ⊠ *Page Break Before.*

The section on the Solar System will now **always** start at the top of a page, no matter what changes you make to the text on the page before it.

—— Widow and orphan control ——

Move to the top of page 4, to the paragraph following the heading **Geology**.

At the moment, the whole of this paragraph is positioned on page 4. (This would be another example of when Keep with Next is needed, because the heading for this paragraph is still on the previous page.)

A similar effect might have been achieved in the case of this document in the current state by typing ⎡Ctrl⎤⎡Enter⎤ immediately before this heading which inserts a **hard page break**. However, the hard page break would remain before the heading regardless of how much text was on the previous page. A keep with next formatting only has an effect if the two paragraphs would have been otherwise split by a soft page break.

🖰 *With the insertion point in this paragraph, use Format Paragraph to clear ⊠ Widow/Orphan Control*

The last line of the paragraph is now by itself on page 4 with the rest of the paragraph now on page 3. The single line at the top of a page in this situation is called an **orphan**. (You can probably imagine the opposite situation, where the first line of a paragraph is on its own at the bottom of a page: this is called a **widow**.)

🖰 *Display the Format Paragraph dialog and check ⊠ Widow/Orphan control again. Click* [**OK**]

Widow/Orphan control follows standard typesetting convention. It does not necessarily keep a paragraph together, but it ensures that no single line of a paragraph is separated from the main body of the paragraph by a page break. It always keeps at least two lines of the paragraph together on each page (unless there are only three or four lines in the paragraph, in which case it will keep the whole paragraph together, as in the example above).

———— Keep lines together ————

🖰 *Add an extra sentence to the end of the paragraph you have been looking at:*

`The existence of the canals was disproved when powerful telescopes were focused on Mars for the first time.`

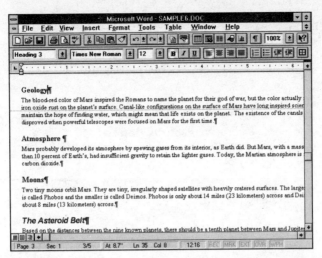

This extra text makes the paragraph four lines long now, and presents you with a new problem. Widow/Orphan control is selected for the paragraph, but it will not prevent the splitting of this paragraph. You want to keep this <u>whole</u> paragraph together on one page. To do this you use the <u>K</u>eep Lines Together option.

🖰 *Place the insertion point somewhere in the paragraph, and check ⊠ <u>K</u>eep Lines Together from the F<u>o</u>rmat <u>P</u>aragraph dialog.*

The paragraph will now be printed all on one page.

Notice that the <u>K</u>eep Lines Together and Keep With Ne<u>x</u>t options work on one paragraph at a time. Selecting several paragraphs and applying the 'together' option applies that option to each one – so that the lines within each would be kept 'together', rather than all the paragraphs being kept 'together'.

———— Inserting a page break ————

Although you have seen many ways which a page break can be caused, there may be situations in which none of these ways

are appropriate but you still want a page break. A page break
may be directly inserted at any given place. Such a page break
is the given the term 'Hard' because, unlike the others, it always remains at the same point in the text in which it was
placed.

*Scroll to the top of the document and position the inser-
tion point before the heading* **Venus***.*

Press Ctrl Enter

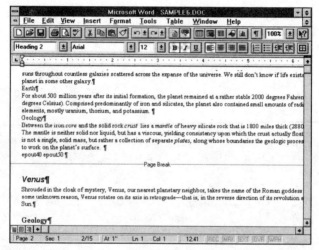

Page breaks can also be inserted from the Insert Break... dialog:

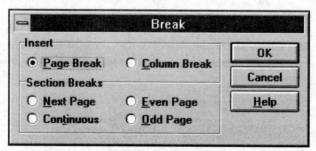

Manual page breaks should be used with restraint. As seen
earlier, Word has several formats to control where automatic
page breaks occur; these should be used in most cases instead

of manual page breaks, as they automatically adjust when text
is added to or deleted from the document.

Summary: Pagination control

- The Format Paragraph Text Flow dialog tab contains four pagination control features:
    - ⊠ Widow/Orphan Control prevents a single line
      from a paragraph being left at the top or bottom
      of a page by ensuring that at least two lines of
      the paragraph are kept together.
    - ⊠ Keep Lines Together keeps the lines making
      up a paragraph together on one page.
    - ⊠ Keep With Next keeps one paragraph to-
      gether with the next one and is most useful
      where headings should be kept with a following
      paragraph.
    - ⊠ Page Break Before forces the selected para-
      graph to be the first on a page. Remember that
      any paragraphs created from such a paragraph
      are also first on a page.
- Manual page breaks can be inserted by pressing
  `Ctrl` `Enter`, or by using the Insert Break dialog, but
  should be used sparingly.

17

—— PAGE SETUP ——

> **This chapter covers:**
> - Using the mouse to change the margin settings.
> - Changing margins, paper size and paper source using the Page Setup dialog.

———— Setting margins using ————
the mouse

🖱 *Go to the top of the document.*

🖱 *Change to page layout view (hint: click* ▦ *next to the horizontal scroll bar).*

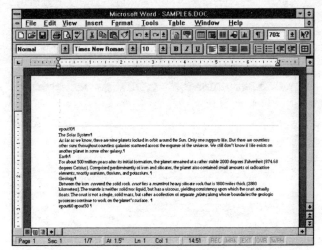

The white area in the centre of the ruler indicates the extent of the page between the margins of the document. This is where text can be entered. The margins can be changed in page layout view simply by dragging the edges of this white area on the ruler.

> ☞ *The grey text saying* **Index** *at the tops of pages in this particular document is to do with headers and footers. You will examine these later.*

🖱 *Position the mouse pointer in the middle of the two indent markers ('triangles')* ⬓ *at the left edge of the white area on the horizontal ruler.*

The mouse pointer shape should now be ↔

👉 *Be careful not to drag the indent markers* ⬓ *by mistake!*

🖱 *Click and drag the markers so that the margin moves to a position approximately 2" from the left edge of the document.*

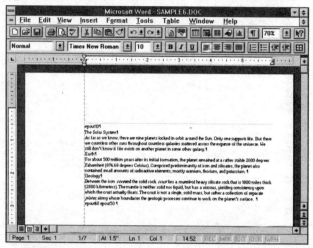

👆 *The number 2 should just be visible in the grey area at the extreme left of the ruler.*

While the margins are being adjusted with the mouse, a dotted grey vertical line appears, indicating the position of the margin as you drag it across. Note that as the margin moves, the white area on the ruler changes size to reflect the changes. It is important to realise that the measurements on the white area always start at the left or bottom margin position, not the edge of the document.

Any of the four margins (left, right, top and bottom) can be moved using a similar technique.

🖱 *Position the mouse pointer at the top edge of the white area on the vertical ruler so that ‡ appears. Click and drag so that the margin is approximately 2" from the top of the document.*

Setting margins using the Page Setup dialog

Using the mouse is an easy way to move the margins, but it isn't always very precise. In order to have more control over the margin positions, you will use the File Page Setup dialog.

🖱️ *Select File Page Setup.*

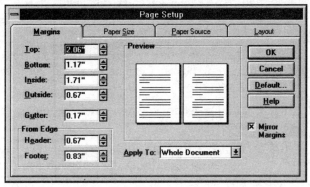

If your screen doesn't look like the above, ensure that the Margins tab is selected at the top of the dialog.

Simply type new values into the appropriate boxes or click the spinners 🔼 to increase or decrease existing values of the margins.

👍 *If you would like the current margin settings to be the default margins when you create a new document (based on the current template), click* Default... *and click* Yes *on the dialog which appears.*

You may be curious about the Gutter. The **gutter** is extra space added to the left (or inside, see below) margins of documents that are to be bound, so that part of the text isn't hidden by the binding. So, an 8.69" wide page with a 1" gutter and 1" left and right margins has 5.69" of printable width remaining.

You might think that the Left margin and gutter perform similar roles. In fact, text can be printed in the left margin (using negative left indents), but never in the gutter area.

The Apply To pull down list allows you to apply margin settings to various parts of the document. The choices in the list are dependent upon whether a selection has been made in the document, i.e. a simple flashing insertion point will give certain choices depending on whether you selected a word or a paragraph. The choices referring to sections will not be available if the document has only one section (as it will unless you have inserted a section). The choices are listed below:

Choices With No Selection Made	
This Point Forward	Dialog settings will affect all text from the current position of the insertion point to the end of the document.
Whole Document	Dialog settings will affect the entire document.
This Section	Dialog settings will affect only the section currently containing the insertion point.
Choices With a Selection	
Selected Text	Dialog settings will affect only the currently selected text.
Whole Document	Dialog settings will affect the entire document.
Selected Sections	Dialog settings will affect the whole of any section that is wholly or partially contained within the current selection.

You would use mirrored margins if you were planning a double-sided document. When ⊠ Mirrored Margins is checked the dialog refers to inside and outside margins (instead of left and right). 'Inside' refers to the margin on each page that will end up next to the binding. 'Outside' refers to the margin on the outer edge of each page (i.e. the bit you would grab to turn the page).

🖱 *Clear ⊠ Mirror Margins.*

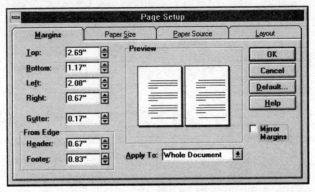

The dialog has changed to reflect single-sided printing. Thus 'Inside' and 'Outside' have now changed to 'Left' and 'Right' and the preview has changed accordingly.

🖱 *Set all four margins to 1.5" using the dialog.*

Paper size

Now that you've specified the margins for the document you will want to look at changing the paper orientation.

Choose the Paper Size tab in the Page Setup dialog.

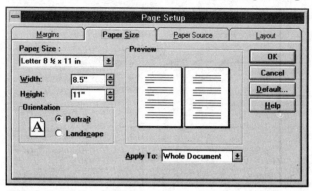

This dialog provides control over Paper Size, Width and Height and the orientations Portrait and Landscape. The Apply To list contains the same choices as detailed above.

Paper Size allows you to specify different paper sizes on which to print. The sizes in this list are based on the printer you are currently using.

Width and Height allow you to specify a custom paper size (by default, it will show the dimensions of the current paper size). Your printer must support whatever width and height you specify – you cannot print 24" x 36" paper from an A4 printer. For this reason, it is usually best to leave these values unchanged and specify paper size through the Paper Size list.

Notice that this page is set up for Letter sized paper. This is a common paper size used in America, and the size which all the Word 6 example files employ. In order to print out any of these examples, you will therefore have to specify A4 paper instead from this dialog.

A portrait page is taller than it is wide (like this book), whereas a landscape page is wider than it is tall.

 Alternate between ⊙ Landscape and ⊙ Portrait to see the preview change orientation.

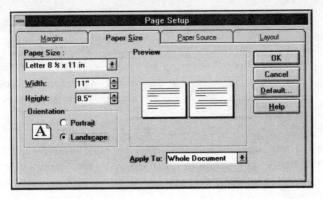

🖰 *Ensure that ⦿ Portrait is on and that the Apply To list shows Whole Document.*

🖰 *Click [OK] to apply the new settings to the document.*

Paper source

🖰 *Choose the Paper Source tab in the Page Setup dialog.*

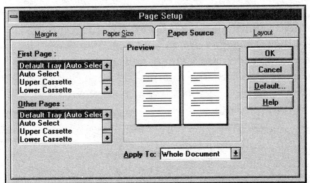

Very often when you're writing a business letter the first page will be printed on headed paper, while the remaining pages are printed on plain or continuation paper. This dialog allows you

to select different trays on your printer (if available) for the
first and remaining pages.

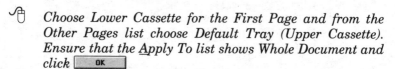 *Choose Lower Cassette for the First Page and from the
Other Pages list choose Default Tray (Upper Cassette).
Ensure that the Apply To list shows Whole Document and
click* OK

☞ *The choices available to you from this dialog are printer specific –
that is, they will change depending upon which type of printer you
are using.*

If you were to print the document now, the first page would be
printed on whatever paper happened to be in the lower tray.

Summary: Document formatting
- The Margins tab on the Page Setup dialog can be
  used to specify the margins (and gutter) exactly for
  various parts of a document.
- The gutter is a portion of each page that is set aside
  for the binding process.
- The Paper Size tab on the Page Setup dialog can be
  used to change the paper size and paper orientation
  for various parts of a document.
- Portrait pages are taller than they are wide. Landscape pages are wider than they are tall.
- The Paper Source tab on the Page Setup dialog can
  be used to specify different paper sources on the current printer.

18

MOVING WITHIN A DOCUMENT

This chapter covers:

- Go To – how to move quickly to different places in the document.
- Bookmarks – how to mark locations in the document.

Go to

You often want to move quickly to certain locations in a document. Word's Go To feature allows you to move to locations in a document in a variety of ways. The Go To... command is accessible from the Edit menu (which gives a dialog), pressing F5, pressing Ctrl G or double-clicking the status bar (which also gives a dialog).

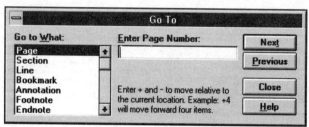

🖰 *Move to the top of the document (⎡Ctrl⎤⎡Home⎤) and choose Edit Go To...*

Imagine that you want to go to the top of page 2.

🖰 *Type 2 into the Enter Page Number box and click* ⎡ Go To ⎤

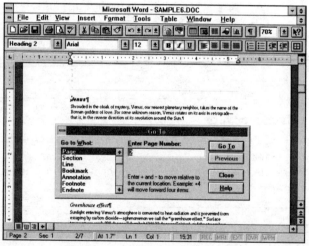

The insertion point is now located at the top of page 2. As you will often be using the Go To feature repeatedly to view your document or to search for a certain position, the dialog remains on-screen until you ⎡ Close ⎤ it.

🖱 *Drag the dialog (using its title bar) to the top of the screen so that it does not obscure the text.*

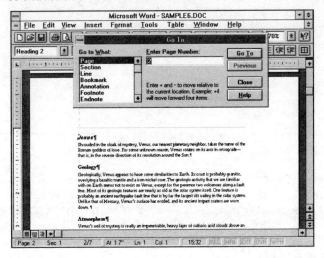

🖱 *Click the Go To dialog title bar to activate the dialog again, and type 3 into the Enter Page Number box. Click* `Go To`

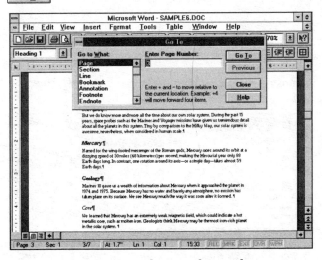

The insertion point moves to the top of page three.

Notice Word's helpful hint about using + and - to move relative amounts. For example, had you typed +3 on the last example you would now be at page 5 (2+3) rather than 3.

 Click Close

Bookmarks

If you were working on a paper document, you might place a bookmark at a place to which you frequently had to return. Word's Bookmark feature allows you to do the equivalent in your electronic document – although as you will see, if you use Word's more advanced featues, an electronic bookmark is far more powerful.

The example you are using already has some bookmarks defined. You will see how they work before defining some of your own.

 If you are not there already, use Ctrl Home *to move to the top of the document.*

 Choose Edit Goto, then choose Bookmark from the Go to What list.

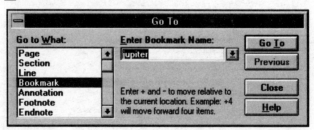

 From the drop down list, choose the name **uranus***.*

Click [**Go To**]

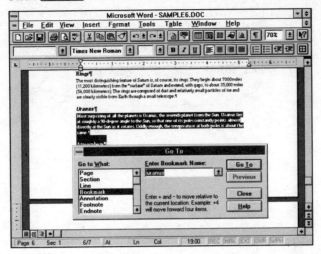

You will observe that the document has jumped to the text following the heading Uranus. This text was previously marked with a bookmark called 'uranus'.

 There is currently no indication in the document of a bookmark anywhere in this paragraph. If you want to be able to see the location of the bookmarks, you will need to go into the Tools Options dialog, choose the View tab and check ☒ Bookmarks. Thereafter, bookmarks will be indicated by a pair of grey square brackets: [ ]

You will now define a bookmark of your own.

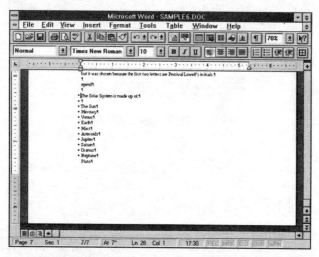

Go to the bottom of the document and position the insertion point in the line `The solar system is made up of`.

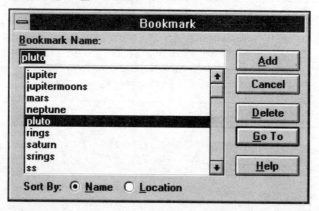

Choose *Edit Bookmark...*

The Bookmark dialog appears. This dialog lists all the bookmarks that exist in this document, and allows you to define a new bookmark by typing in its name.

> ☞ *Notice the Sort By option. The choices are to sort the bookmarks by name (alphabetically), or by bookmark location in the document.*

🖰 *Type* **Solarsystem** *into the* <u>B</u>*ookmark Name box and click* ✕ *to define the bookmark.*

🖰 *Move to the top of the document (* Ctrl Home *).*

You could go to the bookmark you just defined, to check that it works! Use the Go To dialog again, this time accessed in a different way:

🖰 *Double-click in the page number or position sections of the status bar.*

Choose Bookmark in the Go to <u>W</u>*hat list and choose* **so-larsystem** *from the* <u>E</u>*nter Bookmark Name drop-down list. Click* [**Go To**]

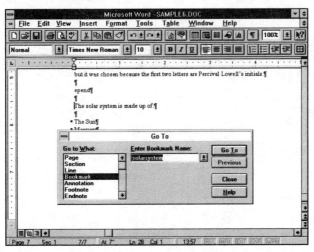

The insertion point has moved back to the position at which you defined your 'solarsystem' bookmark.

🖰 *Close the dialog and the* SAMPLE6.DOC *document.*

Summary: Go to and bookmarks

- Edit Go To..., pressing `F5`, pressing `Ctrl` `G` or double-clicking the page number in the status bar will all bring up the Go To dialog.
- Typing a number into the Go To dialog allows you to go to the beginning of a specific page.
- Bookmarks are defined by positioning the insertion point at a location or selecting a piece of text, choosing Edit Bookmark..., typing a name and choosing `Add`
- Bookmarks can be used as the destination of a Go To command by choosing the name of the bookmark from the Bookmark drop-down list in the Go To dialog.

19

──── TIMESAVERS ────

This chapter covers:
- AutoCorrect.
- AutoText.
- Spellchecking.

──── AutoCorrect and AutoText ────

The AutoText and AutoCorrect features provide ways of storing frequently used pieces of text, graphics, tables, etc. Each allows a piece of text to be converted into something else – typically something shorter or wrong into something which is longer or correct (technically you could arrange for longer text to be abbreviated or for typing errors to be introduced).

There is quite a lot of overlap between the functions of AutoText and AutoCorrect. However there is a difference. AutoCorrect is designed for situations where you always want the same item to be inserted whenever you type a particular word. Typically these might apply to common typing or spelling errors, or to abbreviations. Some examples would be:

- teh should be replaced by **the**
- inc should be replaced by **include**
- jan should be replaced by **January.**

AutoCorrect is triggered automatically when you reach the end of the word, typically by typing Space or Enter. In contrast, AutoText is used for text that should only be replaced when you request it. For example, sometimes OCT should be replaced by **Oxford Computer Training**; on other occasions OCT should remain as OCT.

AutoText can also be used to replace more than one word, so **standard times and conditions** could be replaced with appropriate details.

AutoCorrect

Create a new document. Switch to normal view and choose 100% zoom. Type **teh cat** *('the cat' misspelt).*

As soon as you pressed Space just before **cat**, AutoCorrect sprang into action and corrected your spelling of **the**. This is a built in correction which is already defined in Word.

Try another: type **recieve** *(again misspelt).*

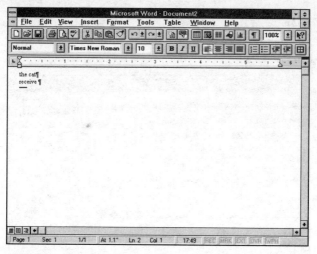

Again, Word has AutoCorrected your misspelling.

Imagine that you want to create an AutoCorrect entry such that every time you typed **addr** Word inserted your name and address. First you need to create the AutoCorrect entry:

Type your name and address. Apply some formatting, e.g. italic and right aligned. Then select the whole name and address.

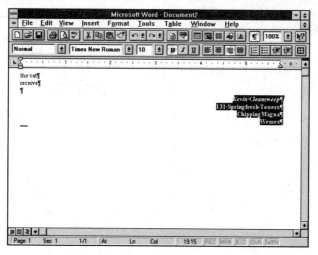

Now you can define the name and address as an AutoCorrect entry **addr** (for address):

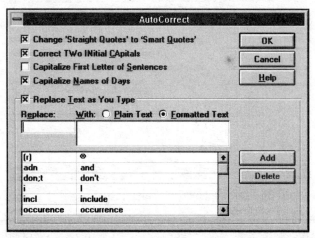

Choose AutoCorrect... from the Tools menu.

Your selected text should appear in the With box in the centre of the dialog, but because it is formatted as right-aligned, you cannot see it (it is currently positioned at the 'invisible' right hand edge of the page!).

Although you actually want the formats included as part of the AutoCorrect text, it makes sense to ignore the format temporarily so you can see the text.

🖰 *Click ⦿ Plain Text*

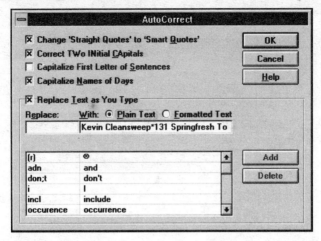

In the middle of the dialog you will now see your selected text and a blank Replace edit box waiting for an AutoCorrect name.

🖰 *Switch back to ⦿ Formatted Text. Type* **addr** *into the Replace box. Click* [**Add**]

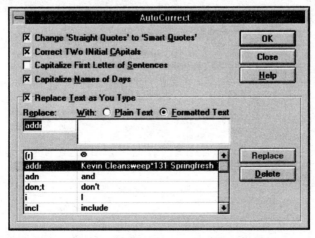

The lower part of this dialog shows the abbreviations currently defined and the items used to replace them. Your new entry, **addr**, has been inserted at the appropriate point (alphabetical) in the list. You can also see that **adn** is already defined as **and, teh** is defined as **the**.

🖰 *Scroll down as necessary to see the entry for* **teh***. Click*
[OK] *to close the AutoCorrect dialog.*

🖰 *Use* [Ctrl] [End] *to move to the end of the document. Press* [Enter] *to leave a few blank lines and type* **addr** [Space]

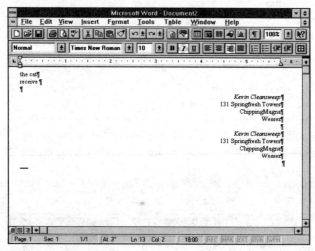

As soon as you press [Space] at the end of **addr**, your full, formatted address appears, replacing the typed text.

Smart quotes and capitals

Other functions of AutoCorrect are to ensure that words are correctly capitalised and that quotes ('speech marks') are correctly paired.

Click 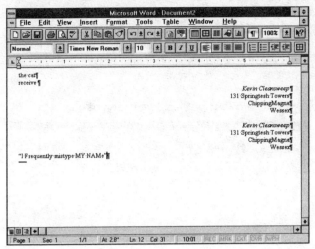 *and type* '*i FRequently mistype* MY NAMe'

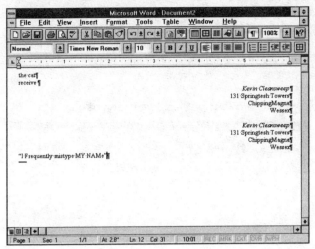

Notice that Word has corrected your typing to read 'I Frequently mistype MY NAMe'.

There are several points to note here:

- Word has corrected i to I — this is an AutoCorrect entry:

Choose AutoCorrect... from the Tools menu.

The fifth entry in the Replace list is Replace i with I.

- Word has corrected standard ' quotes to SmartQuotes ' '. This feature is controlled by the checkbox ⊠ Change Straight Quotes to Smart Quotes.

- Word has corrected the capitalisation of certain words. Words with only the first two letters capitalised (a common typing error) are corrected to have only the first letter capitalised e.g. FRequently. Words with more than two capitals typed are assumed to be deliberate and are not corrected e.g. MY NAMe.

Click Cancel *to close the AutoCorrect dialog.*

AutoText

An AutoText entry is used when an abbreviation is only replaced in certain instances, e.g. sometimes OCT is to be replaced by **Oxford Computer Training**; on other occasions OCT should remain as OCT.

Type **Oxford Computer Training** *and select it.*

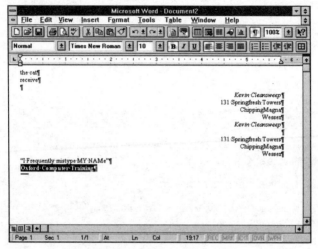

Choose AutoText... from the Edit menu.

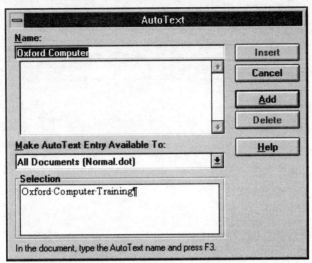

This dialog is similar to the AutoCorrect dialog. In the upper half of the dialog are listed any currently defined AutoText entries (note that Word is not supplied with predefined entries, unlike the AutoCorrect facility); in the lower box is the current selection. You want to define the name OCT:

 *Type **OCT** in the **N**ame box and click* Add

Press Ctrl End *to move to the end of the document. Press* Enter *to leave a few blank lines and type* OCT Space

Notice that in contrast to the AutoCorrect entry the AutoText entry is **not** inserted automatically by finishing the word with Space.

🖰 *Move the insertion point into OCT, then click the AutoText button 🖳 (or press F3).*

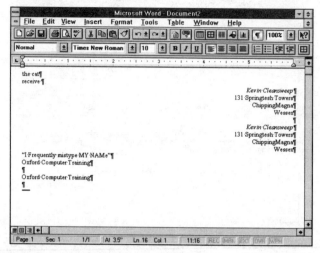

It is not important whether you typed OCT in capital letters or not – AutoText entries are not case sensitive.

👆 *If the computer beeps when you click 🖳 and the message 'The specified text is not a valid AutoText name' is displayed in the status bar, ensure that the insertion point is on (or immediately after) the AutoText name and click 🖳 again.*

Managing AutoText and AutoCorrect entries

Deleting entries

AutoText/Correct entries, once defined, can be deleted by using the [Delete] button in the AutoText/Correct dialogs.

🖰 *Choose AutoText... from the Edit menu, select OCT and click* [Delete] *Click* [Close]

The OCT AutoText entry has been deleted.

To verify this, leave a blank line, type OCT and click 🖳

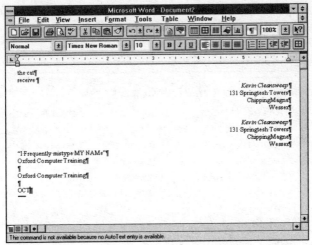

> 🖎 *The message in the status bar will be slightly different if you have one or more AutoText entries remaining after you have deleted the OCT entry. In this case the message will refer to how to create an entry for AutoText.* **'The specified text is not a valid AutoText name. Use Edit AutoText to create AutoText entries.'**

 Close the document.

Saving entries

AutoText/Correct entries will be saved for use at later times and with other documents when you close Word.

> 🖎 *AutoCorrect entries are always stored in NORMAL.DOT, the normal template; AutoText may be stored either in NORMAL.DOT or another specified template*

Adding AutoCorrect entries automatically

Whilst you can add AutoCorrect entries manually, you can also add entries corrected by spellchecking. This is covered in the next section.

Summary: AutoText and AutoCorrect

- AutoText (known as 'Glossaries' in Word for Windows 2.0) and AutoCorrect provide timesaving ways of inserting frequently used items and correcting common typing mistakes.
- AutoText is most appropriate for items that are only needed infrequently and for items that are not always replaced.
- To define an AutoText entry, select the item, choose Edit AutoText..., type a suitable name and click [Add].
- To use an AutoText entry type the abbreviated name and click 🖫 (or press F3).
- AutoCorrect is suitable for items that must always be replaced, such as common typing mistakes.
- To define an AutoCorrect entry, select the item, choose Tools AutoCorrect, type a suitable name and click [Add].
- AutoCorrect entries will automatically be inserted by Word when you press Space at the end of an incorrect word for which it has an AutoCorrect entry.

Spell checking

As well as using AutoCorrect to correct particular misspelt words, Word has a built-in spell checker which can work through your document and compare all the words against an inbuilt dictionary. The spell checker stops when it finds a word it does not recognise, and suggests a possible replacement.

Create your own paragraph of a few sentences including some obvious spelling mistakes. Do not use common errors like 'teh' and 'recieve' as these will be corrected by AutoCorrect.

In the example screenshots the paragraph will be 'You will understand that as the arrangements must take account of the very special dietery requirments of the animal concerned, we have had to arrange special passage. No reputable wildlife organisation would deal with us anyway. Single ticket to Slough from Kidlington, Oxfordshire £6.40.
Aninal foodstuffs £3.55'

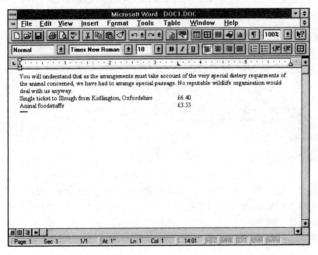

Now you can use the spell checker to correct your misspellings.

Spellchecking button

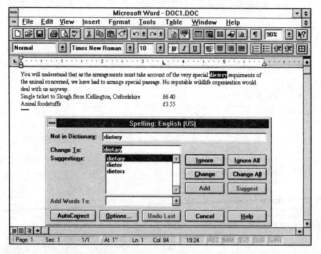

Move the insertion point to the beginning of your incorrectly spelt paragraph and click ☑ on the Standard toolbar.

Word starts an automatic spell check of the document.

The spellchecker will pick up your first misspelled word; in our example, it is 'dietery'. Notice that the speller selects the misspelt word and scrolls the document behind the spelling dialog so that you can see the word's context. If you need more space to see the context of the word, you can move the spelling dialog by dragging it by its title bar.

Practise moving the Spelling dialog so you can see that this works.

In this case, Word may have suggested some words which may be alternatives to the word you misspelled. Possible replacements for the word meant by 'dietery' are shown in the dialog box.

You can select (click on) the correctly spelt word from the suggestions list (which places it into the Change To box), or you can type it directly into the Change To box. To replace the misspelt word with the word in the Change To box:

Click **Change** *(with the correct spelling selected). (Double-clicking the correct spelling in the Suggestions list would have had the same effect).*

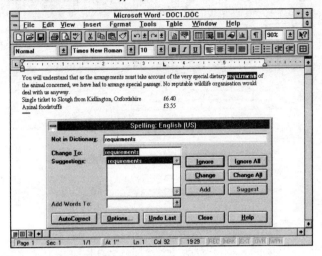

Word has replaced 'dietery' with 'dietary'.

👍 *If you think you may have misspelt the same word elsewhere, you can choose* **Change All** *instead of* **Change** *. This changes all the instances of the misspelt word everywhere in the document.*

Word has now moved on to the next misspelling ('requirments'). This time, only a single alternative is suggested – 'requirements'.

Click [Change] *to replace the error with the correct spelling and continue spell checking the rest of the document, changing words as necessary. Pause if you reach a spelling for which Word cannot produce a suggestion; e.g.* `Kidlington`. *in this example.*

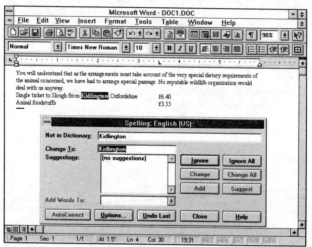

Proper nouns are not always recognised. If the word is not a proper noun, then it is of a type that Word does not have a close approximation to, e.g. abbreviations. In these cases, you would simply check the spelling by eye and click [Ignore] if it's correct. If not, you would type the correct spelling in the Change To box and click [Change].

If you send a lot of animals to Kidlington, and you don't want the word to be picked up every time by the spelling checker, you can add it to a **custom dictionary**.

Custom dictionaries

Word allows you to keep as many custom dictionaries as you like: if you were a doctor, you might want a dictionary containing words like pneumonoultramicroscopicsilicovolcanoconiosis, but not necessarily all the time. You are therefore allowed to choose a dictionary to match the type of document you are checking. If you have several dictionaries on your system, you can select the one to use from the pull-down list next to Add <u>W</u>ords To.

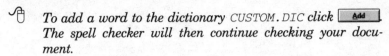 *To add a word to the dictionary* CUSTOM.DIC *click* [**Add**]. *The spell checker will then continue checking your document.*

Adding words to AutoCorrect

If you misspell a word frequently, you can use the spelling checker to add a misspelt word and it's replacement to AutoCorrect, so that the spelling will be automatically corrected in future.

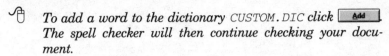 *To add an entry to AutoCorrect, make sure the replacement word is in the Change <u>T</u>o box, and then click* [**AutoCorrect**]. *Word will then continue the spell check.*

Finish spell checking your document, and then:

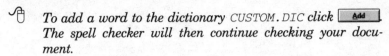 *Close the document, saving changes.*

Summary: Spell Checking

- Word offers a powerful spelling checker, activated by clicking 🗹 in the toolbar.
- You can perform automatic checking of the entire document, or check a single word by selecting it and then clicking 🗹
- When a word is not found in the dictionary, Word displays it and a list of alternative suggestions. You can then type an alternative, ignore it (perhaps a proper noun) or add it to a custom dictionary for future use.
- You can have any number of specialised custom dictionaries.

20

TABLES

This chapter covers:

- Reasons for using tables.
- The Table Wizard: semi-automatic table creation.
- How to insert a table.
- Selection within a table.
- Entering data in a table and formatting.
- Modifying a table.
- Applying a border in a table.

Why use tables?

People often ask 'do I need to know how to use tables if I don't handle numbers?' The answer is 'yes'! Tables are useful not only for numeric data, but also for text in a variety of situations, such as:

- minutes of meetings
- film scripts
- fax coversheets

You will see that tables have various benefits over the use of tabs to produce even the simplest document:

- Within each cell of a table, text wordwraps
- Tables preserve 'row integrity'; i.e. information on each row stays together
- Tables are very easy to adjust

——————— Using the Table Wizard ———————

Word provides a **wizard** to help you create tables. A wizard helps you to create a complex table by taking you through a series of simple steps. The result may be manually altered later as necessary.

The options offered by the wizard are somewhat limited, but simple to use. Let's begin with a typical table of figures.

Suppose you want to create a table which shows monthly sales figures for two salesmen, each selling two product groups:

	Steven Sharpsuit		Kevin Cleansweep	
	Vacuum Cleaners	Kitchen	Vacuum Cleaners	Kitchen
Jan	232.34	34.45	354.56	765.45
Feb	12.40	975.30	123.45	345.76
Mar	543.67	234.45	456.67	342.65
Apr	345.76	123.56	3.54	267.54
May	234.65	43.65	645.76	347.76
Jun	67.76	3.54	453.65	323.65
Jul	44.70	234.54	543.67	234.45
Aug	566.70	7.53	345.75	123.56
Sep	23.65	978.76	345.76	9.55
Oct	9.78	645.76	23.65	34.76
Nov	43.45	623.65	23.65	978.76
Dec	45.765	754.34	9.78	645.76

Create a new document and choose <u>I</u>nsert Table... from
the T<u>a</u>ble menu.

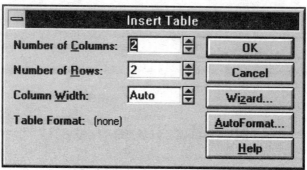

You will see more of this dialog later. For the time being:

Click Wi<u>z</u>ard...

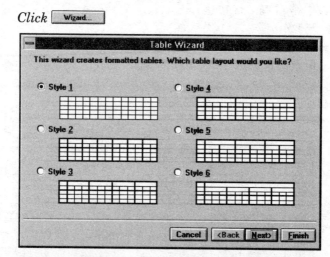

This is the first of six pages of the Table Wizard that will guide
you through defining the table size, applying headings and
aligning the data. The choice here is what layout do you want.

Choose ⊙Style <u>2</u> and click Next>

The subsequent pages of the wizard vary slightly according to
the table style that you specified. The choice here is clear
enough — you are shown a sample in the chosen style and
asked how many columns you want.

Click ⬇ to drop down the list of suitable sizes.

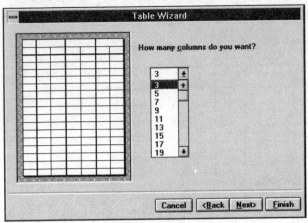

Notice that for your chosen style you must have an odd number of columns: the first column plus subsequent pairs.

Choose 5 and click Next›

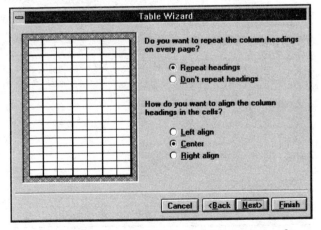

The table you create may split to several pages and you want the headings (in the top few rows) to be repeated on every new page that the table goes onto. You might also want the column headings to be centred in the columns.

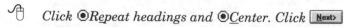
Click ⊙*Repeat headings* and ⊙*Center*. Click Next>

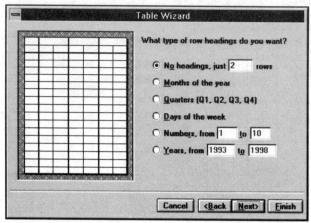

You are now being asked to choose row headings (not column headings).

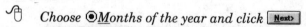
Choose ⊙*Months of the year* and click Next>

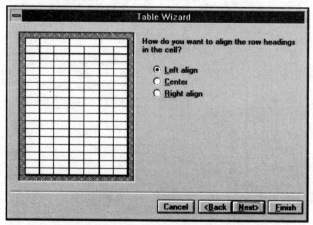

You might want your new headings to be left aligned:

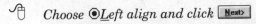

Choose ◉*Left align and click* [Next>]

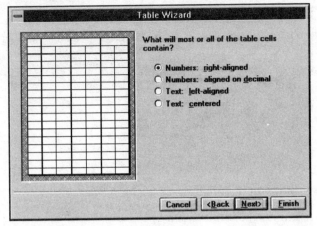

What default alignment do you want for the contents of cells in the table (obviously excluding row and column headings that we've just defined)? You are going to put sales figures into the table and so alignment on the decimal point would seem to be a good option.

Choose ◉*Numbers: aligned on decimal and click* [Next>]

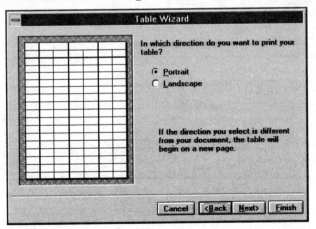

For our example the page with the table should be in the normal (portrait) orientation. Landscape orientation is particularly useful for very wide tables.

🖑 *Choose ⦿Portrait and click* Next>

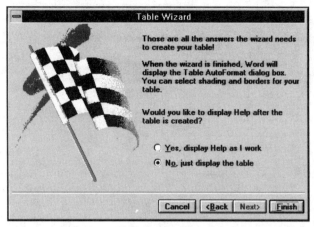

This is the last page of the wizard, asking if you want on-line help.

🖑 *Choose ⦿No, just display the table and click* Finish

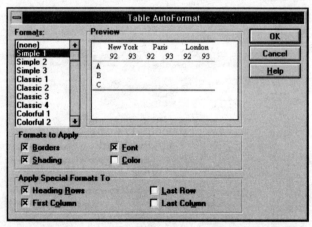

After the wizard has finished you are offered the Table Auto-Format dialog in order to choose one of many preset formats.

Experiment with some of the Formats if you like – you can see a sample in the preview window. Finally choose Grid 3 and click OK

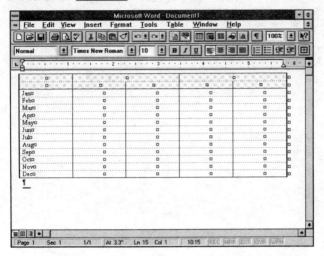

If you don't have the table gridlines visible on the screen, select Table Gridlines. If you don't have the paragraph markers, press ¶ on the toolbar as this often makes navigating a table easier.

Finally, to finish the table

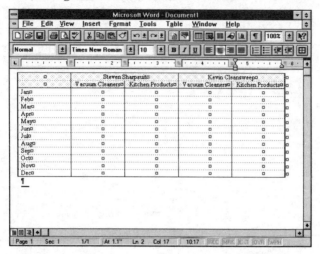

Type Steven Sharpsuit, Kevin Cleansweep, Vacuum Cleaners *and* Kitchen Products *into the appropriate cells, using* Tab *to move between the cells.*

Inserting a table manually

There are two ways of creating a table in Word:

- create the table and then type data into it
- select some existing data and insert a table around it.

The first is the usual method if you have not typed the data. If you already have the data, Word can convert it into a table for you

As you do not have any data to convert, you will set up a simple table for a delivery notice, and type the data directly into the table.

🖰 *Press* `Ctrl` `End` *to move to the end of the document. Then, insert three blank lines.*

First of all, type in a heading for this table:

`White Rabbit Couriers`

`'We're Always Late!'`

`Delivery Notice:`

🖰 *Add some appropriate formatting to this title.*

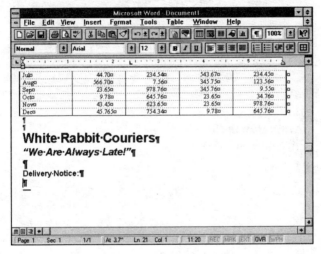

——— Insert table button ———

You are now going to set up a table into which you can type the delivery details.

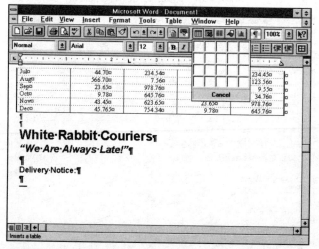 *Click ▦ on the Standard toolbar.*

The white gridded square that appears is a request for you to tell Word how big you'd like the new table to be. (If you'd like the square to go away, you can click the word 'Cancel' at the bottom of the square, click ▦ again or press `Esc`.) To specify a table size (in terms of numbers of rows and columns) click and hold down the mouse button inside the square, then drag downwards and rightwards watching the figures change at the bottom of the square. When the desired dimensions are shown, release the mouse button.

Click and hold down the mouse button inside the box. Drag downwards and rightwards and watch as the dimensions changes (continue to hold the mouse button).

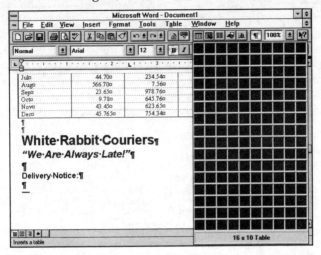

The example above shows a table of 16 rows by 10 columns.

Adjust the mouse position to achieve a '10 x 3 Table', then release the mouse button.

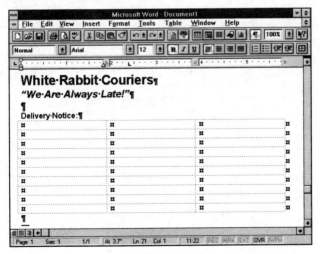

If you don't have table gridlines as shown above, you can select
Gridlines from Table menu.

The grid should mark out the 10 rows and 3 columns for the
table that you have defined. The size of the **cells** (boxes) has
been set by Word automatically: the height of the rows depends
on the current font – being sufficient for one line of text; the
width of the cells is simply the available space divided by the
number of columns, in this case three. Note that the gridlines
shown are for guidance only and will not be printed, although it
is possible to add printable cell **borders** if you wish (see later).

Now that you have defined your table you can enter text into it.
Some useful keystrokes for moving in tables are:

Tab	• moves the insertion point from cell to cell, forwards through the table. • In the last cell on a row automatically moves to the first cell on the next row. • When the insertion point is in the last (lower right) cell of the table, will add another row to the table.
Shift Tab	• moves the insertion point from cell to cell, backwards through the table.

🖰 *Click in the first (upper left) cell and type the heading*
Description

🖰 *Press* Tab *to move one cell to the right and enter the heading* Quantity. *Then press* Tab *again and enter the heading* Part Number *in the upper right cell. Pressing* Tab *again will move the insertion point to the next row.*

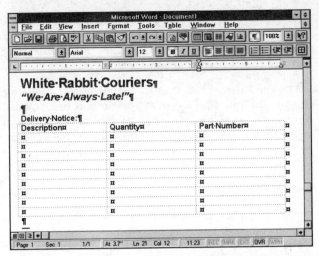

You can start to fill in some of the cells immediately below the headings. ...

Add the information into the appropriate cells by typing the following (starting in the cell below Description):

Croquet Mallets Tab 10 Tab FG5 Tab Croquet Balls
Tab

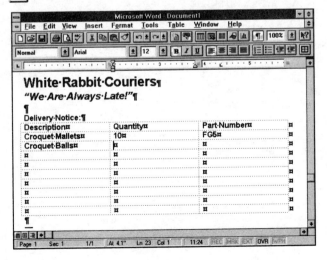

When you get to the word `Hedgehogs` shortly, you might feel that further explanation is necessary. Croquet balls are of course hedgehogs as all readers of *Alice in Wonderland* will know; but the receiver may not know this.

Each cell in the table is like a miniature document with its own formats and you will find that, just as in a full document, you can extend your text by typing until wordwrap starts a new line for you or you can press Enter to start a new paragraph.

With the insertion point positioned after the `s` *in* `Croquet Balls`*, press* Enter

You should find that the 'paragraph' has been ended in the usual way, and that the cell height has expanded automatically.

Type `(Hedgehogs)` *on this new line.*

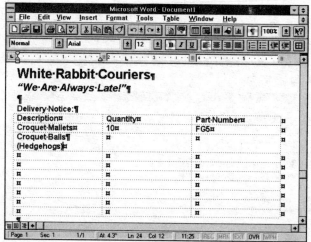

Enter the rest of the data so that the table looks like this:

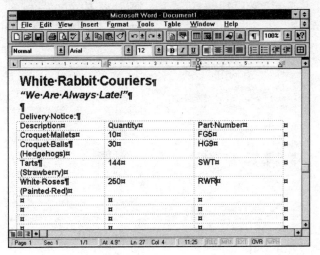

Selection in tables

There are various modifications that you may now want to make to your table but the first you are going to get rid of the unused rows. (In a delivery note you might simply prefer to leave them empty).

First you will need to select the rows to be removed. There are a variety of ways to select cells in a table and you will look at the most straightforward of these.

 Try selecting the word **Quantity** *(hint: double-click the word) and italicise it (hint: click* **I** *).*

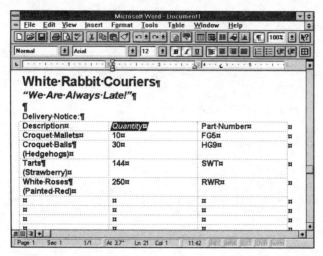

Notice that the black selection is only on the word and **does not fill the cell**.

You can select a complete single cell. Remember that earlier we said each cell is like a miniature document – this extends to having its own selection area. So the mouse pointer will switch to ⇗ at several locations as you move across the table.

⟍ *Click in the cell selection area of the first (`Description`) cell.*

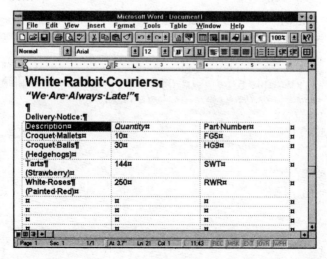

Notice that in this case, the selection is the **whole cell**, in contrast to selecting the text. Actually, there is another way this can be achieved. By starting in any of the text and dragging to the right-hand edge of the cell – Word 'guesses' (using the Intellisense feature) that you want the whole cell and selects it.

Click the middle of the word `Quantity` *and drag the mouse to the right-hand edge of the current cell. As you approach the edge, Word selects the cell for you.*

You can select a range of cells by clicking on a corner cell and dragging across the range to the diagonally opposite corner.

Practice selecting multiple cells.

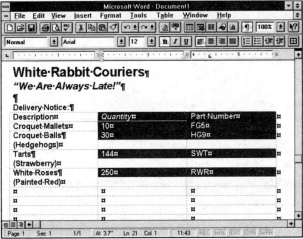

To select multiple rows, click and drag in the leftmost selection area (to the left of the table).

Select the first row (containing the headers) by clicking in the leftmost selection area. Then click **B** *and* **I** *to embolden and italicise the headings. Click* ☰ *to centre the headings.*

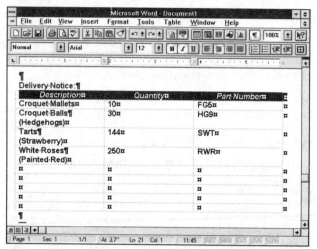

You can also easily select multiple columns, by going to the top gridline of the first column you want to select, and a ↓ pointer should appear. Click and drag across the columns you want. If the top of the column is not visible you may find it easier to choose Table Select Column.

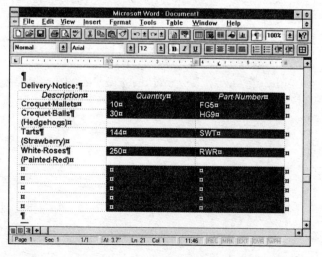

Modifying a table

Now you could remove the superfluous last few rows.

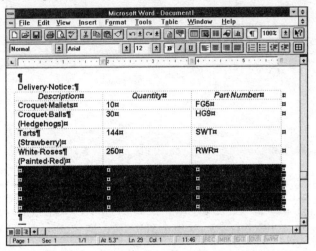 *Click and drag in the leftmost selection area to select the five empty rows at the end of the table.*

And then, to delete the selected rows you can use Delete Rows on the Table menu or the right-click shortcut.

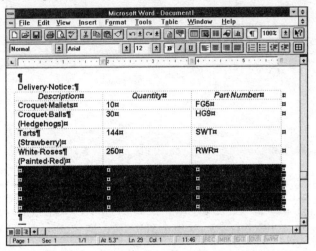 *Right-click the selected rows and choose Delete Rows from the menu.*

You should now have a table looking something like this:

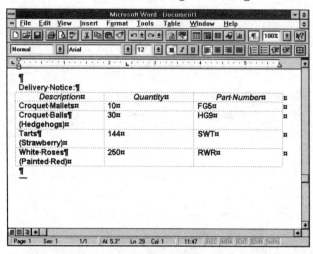

You may be wondering what would have happened if you had pressed [Del] instead of choosing Delete Rows. Had there been any text in the selected rows, it would have been deleted, but the rows would have remained, you can test this:

🖱 *Select the first (heading) row and press* [Del]

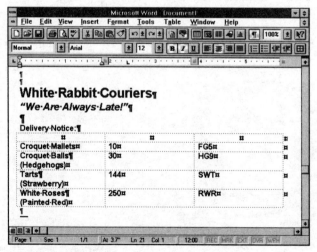

🖱 *Then click* [↶] *to replace the headings.*

The table now looks a little better but the columns are a little too wide for the information contained in them.

Changing table column widths

You will probably have already noticed that when the insertion point is inside the table the ruler displays a set of table column width markers (▥) at the boundaries of each column.

🖰   *Make sure the insertion point is the table.*

The ruler should now show markers like the following: ▥

You can move the ▥ markers by dragging them to new locations and thereby change the widths of the columns for the table as a whole. This is very convenient.

In this example you want to make all the columns narrower:

🖰   *Drag the leftmost* ▥ *to 3" on the ruler, drag the middle* ▥
to 4" and the rightmost ▥ *to 5.5".*

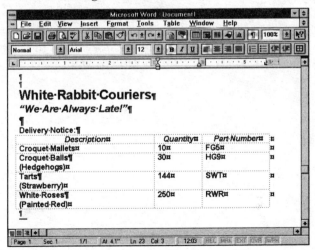

If you prefer you can also change the column widths by dragging when the ⁌⊩⁌ pointer is seen on the column gridlines as shown below:

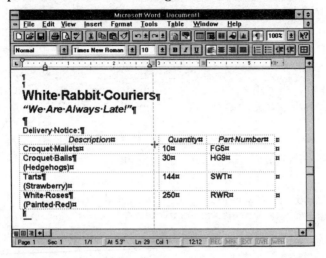

Table borders

Word allows you to set borders of a different style for every cell in your table. Remember that the gridlines you can see on the screen now are simply for your convenience and will not print.

🖰 *Click* ⊞

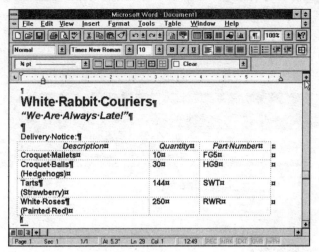

⊞ turns on the borders toolbar.

🖰 *Make sure that the insertion point is flashing inside one of the cells in the table and experiment with* ▢, ▢, ▢, ▢ *on the new toolbar.*

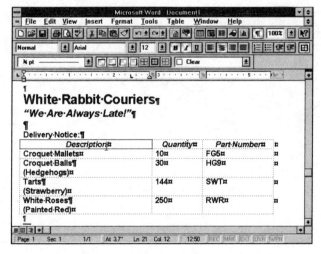

🖰 *Move to a new cell and click* ⊞

Clearly the 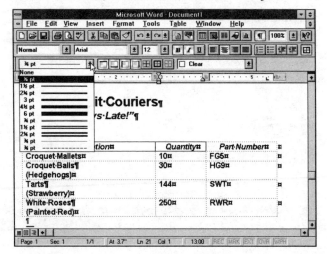 button is a much quicker way of applying all the outside cell borders.

What about different line styles?

🖱 *Click the drop-down list button ± on the line style tool,*
¾ pt ————— ±, to see the available line styles.

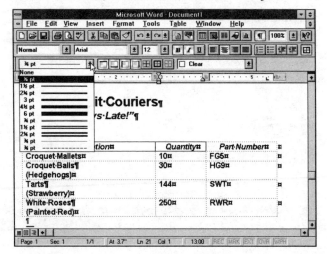

🖱 *Pick a style, e.g. the 1½ pt double line, by clicking it.*

Notice that existing lines have not changed.

🖱 *Move to a new cell and click* 🔲

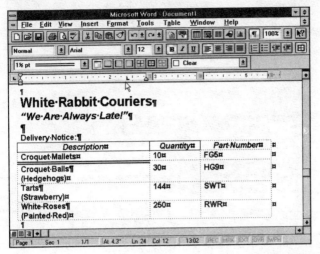

Choosing a new line style only affects subsequently applied lines.

In principle, you could format each cell individually, but in practice you would normally select an area and then apply a certain border type to that selection.

A quick way to select the entire table is by choosing the Select Table command on the Table menu.

🖱 *Select the entire table by using the Table Select Table command.*

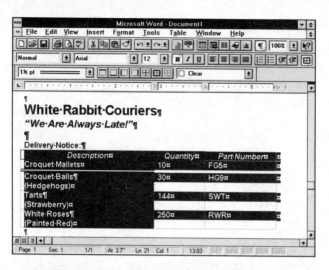

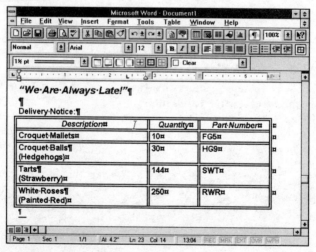

Click ▣ (Outside Border) and ⊞ (Inside Border) and click in the table to remove the selection.

Clicking ▣ adds a border surrounding selected cells whereas clicking ⊞ adds a border between the cells of a table.

In order to emphasise the headings, you might want to apply a thicker border to the bottom of those cells:

🖱 *Select the top row by clicking in the selection area to its left, choose a 3pt single line from the line style dropdown and then click* ▢

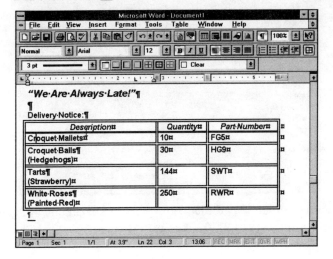

———— Table AutoFormat ————

The table AutoFormat feature is a very easy way to format a table. You have already used this feature: it was chosen automatically with the Table Wizard. Let's see how AutoFormat can be used on the table:

🖱 *Choose Table Auto*__F__*ormat... from the T*__a__*ble menu.*

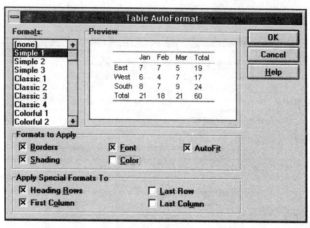

As you have seen this dialog before, just experiment with some of the options, clicking [OK] to apply those options to the table.

For example, try the **Simple3** style:

🖱 *Double-click* **Simple3**. *Then turn off the gridlines using* T__a__*ble* __G__*ridlines and turn off the non-printing characters by clicking* ¶ *(show/hide).*

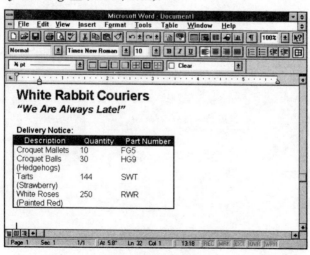

Formatting text in cells

Formatting text in cells is the same as formatting normal text. You have already seen the use of bold and italics in cells, these are examples of font formatting. You saw the use of ▣ to apply centre paragraph alignment. You can also apply other paragraph formats cells, which may be vital if you are using a table as a neat way of arranging minutes or other text documents. Again, word treats the cell as a miniature document: so other than a few problems that a crowded ruler might give – the techniques are the same

You can use the ruler bar to change the margin settings for cells. For example, you could change the left margin indent for the data in the Part Number column of your table.

🖰 *Select these cells.*

You will notice that the ruler above the column now shows markers for the area of the cells within which the text will flow.

🖰 *Use the 🖆 markers on the ruler to drag in the left margin indent for these cells.*

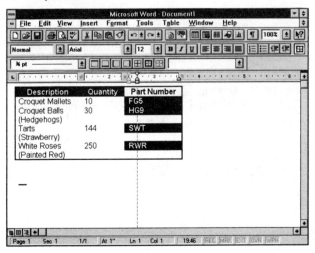

The text within these columns should now be indented from the edge of the cells (notice that the width of the cells has not changed).

Summary: Tables

- Tables have various benefits: wordwrap within cells, row integrity, ease of resizing.
- The Table Wizard makes creation of certain standard tables simple.
- To insert a table manually: click the ▦ button on the standard toolbar and then drag out a size for the new table.
- Within a table you select text in the usual way.
- Select a cell by clicking in the cell selection area.
- Select a range of cells by clicking in the first cell and dragging to the final cell.
- Select a column using the ↓ pointer.
- Select a row using the leftmost selection area.
- Having selected a row or column delete it by using the right-click shortcut menu or drag the ▦ to change table column widths.
- Formatting in cells is the same as formatting normal text.
- Table gridlines by default do **not** print unless you format them to do so using the Borders toolbar, found by clicking ▦
- Table AutoFormat can be used to format table borders to several preset designs.

21

——— TEMPLATES ———

This chapter covers:
- The purpose of templates.
- Using pre-defined templates.
- Using document wizards.
- Creating and using a simple template.

——— What is a template? ———

A template is a 'blueprint' for a document that is used as a base for producing other documents. Every Microsoft Word document must be based on a template although the most commonly used template contains no text and you tend not to notice it. Clicking the New Document tool ⬚, produces a document based on this 'normal' template called NORMAL.DOT. Notice that this filename has a special ending, .DOT to indicate that it is template and not a document.

If you frequently write formal business letters that follow roughly the same style, you could set up a template to include:

- The preferred font that you always use, e.g. Arial 12pt.
- The margin and paper size.
- Your name and address, positioned in the correct place.
- The general outline, e.g. Dear Sir ... Yours faithfully.
- Other text that will be included in every letter.

To create a template, you first create a document containing all of the standard features that will be common to the letters: you must be careful not to include items that will change from letter to letter. The document is then saved in a special manner to create a template or 'blueprint' of it. Then, when new documents are created, they can be based on this template if required. Each time the template is chosen, a copy is made and the original remains unchanged, ready for reuse whenever it is needed. This is analogous to the 'real world' idea of photocopying an empty form and completing the copy, thus leaving the original intact.

Clearly, templates can be great time-savers. As well as being able to create your own templates, you can use pre-defined ones that come supplied with Word. These will be considered here.

Pre-defined templates

There are two different types of template already included with Microsoft Word: wizards and templates. A wizard is a special template that helps you to create a document by taking you through the steps and asking questions about the kind of document you would like to create. By doing this, a wizard makes you concentrate on one decision at a time, helping you to produce more stylish documentation. A template produces a copy of itself and what it contains without the steps of a wizard.

You will look at a simple memo template first in order to gain an understanding of templates, then you will look at the Letter Wizard and use it to produce a standard business letter document.

Creating a document using a template

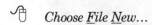 *Choose File New...*

The Template List gives a list of all templates currently found by Word and the Description area gives a short indication of the purpose of the currently selected template. The currently selected template is Normal, which is the default template upon which new documents are based. All the documents you have created until now have been based on this template.

Choose the Memo1 template.

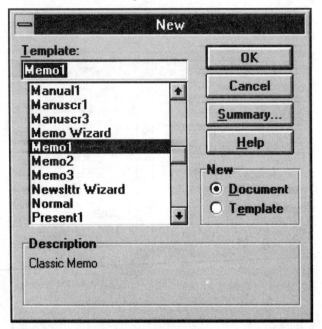

The Description area has updated and is now showing a description for Memo1. Do not be tempted to change the New option to ⊙ Template. This would create a new template based on an old template, in this case Memo1.

 Click ▭ **OK** ▭ *to create a new document based on the Memo1 template.*

For clarity, change the zoom to 100% (if necessary).

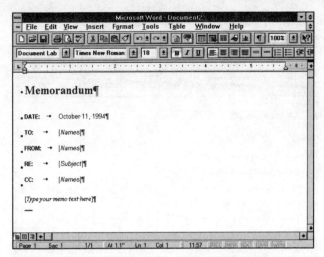

This is a new document based on the Memo1 template. Notice the default text on the page. There are also new **styles** available for this document. You will see more about styles in the next chapter.

Using a template is straightforward: you simply compose your text in the usual way. Text such as **[Names]** is simply a place-marker to enter a list of names. Select the place-marker and type the list of names:

Type some information into the spaces provided in the memo.

Your finished memo might look something like this:

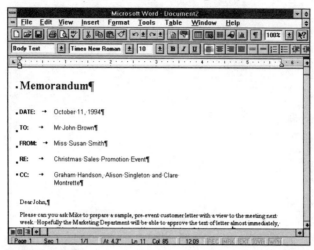

Notice how the different areas of text have been formatted using different styles. This is not something you had to do yourself, since all such information was stored in the template.

Using a wizard template

You first looked at wizards in Chapter 20 when you looked at tables. A wizard takes you through a process step-by-step, giving you structured questions at each stage, finally presenting you with a finished product. Most frequently, as here, wizards are used for formatting. You will use a wizard to format (and help you write) a standard letter complaining to a customer that their cheque had not cleared.

🖰 *Choose File New... and select the Template Letter Wizard.*

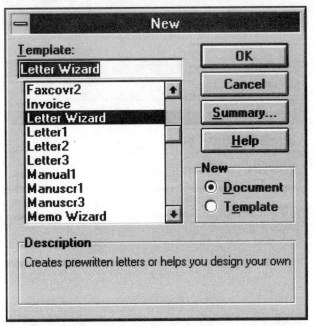

🖰 *Click* `OK`

What follows is six dialogs that take you step-by-step through the process of composing a letter.

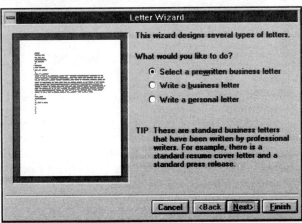

Accept the default, in this case:

🖑 *Choose to ◉ Select a prewritten business letter.*

Click `Next>`

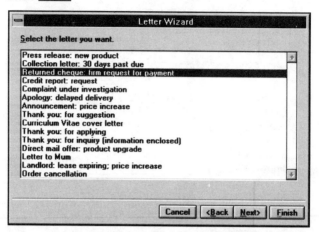

🖑 *Choose the Returned cheque option and click* `Next>`

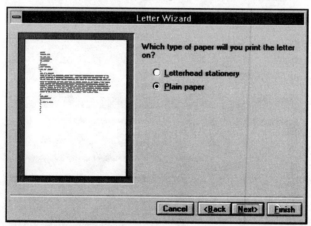

The choice here is whether or not to use letterhead stationery. If you choose ◉ Letterhead stationery the next dialog would ask you about size and position of the letterhead.

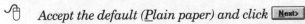 *Accept the default (Plain paper) and click* [Next>]

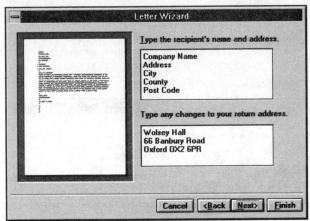

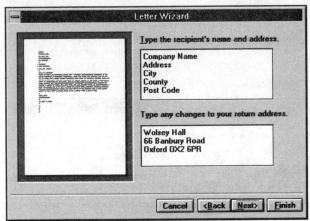 *Type in a name and address for the recipient. If necessary change the sender's details too. Press* [Enter] *to start a new line.*

👍 *Word gets the sender's details from the UserInfo tab in the Tools Options dialog. Set your name and address correctly here for future use.*

 Click [Next>]

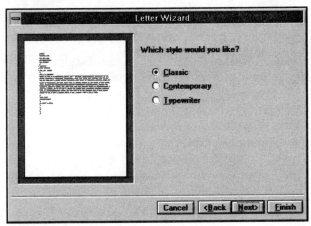

This dialog allows you to choose a 'feel' for the letter: do you want to use a 'classic', 'contemporary' or 'typewriter' style? The main features of each of these styles are:

Classic means a traditional layout with a serif font (Times New Roman)

Contemporary uses a sans serif font (Arial)

Typewriter uses a Courier font to emulate a typewriter.

🖰   *Choose ◉ Classic and click* [Next>]

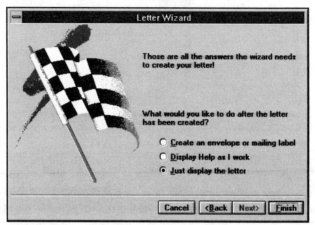

This final dialog indicates that you have nearly finished.

🖰   *Accept the default option (Just display the letter) and click*
[Finish]

After a pause, during which Word is generating the letter, the prewritten letter is presented on the screen.

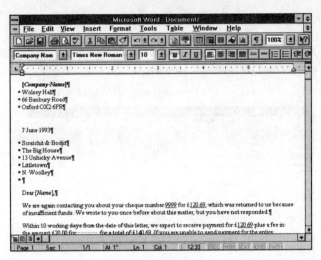

At this stage, add the final details necessary before saving and printing:

🖱 *Change the place-marker [CompanyName] to Aardvark Computers plc and change [Name] to Mr Scrooge.*

Make any other alterations that you feel appropriate. Save the letter and print it.

Creating a template

You have seen how to use predefined templates that are supplied with Word. By this stage you're probably asking if you can change the layout of the letter or alter the way in which the memo is formatted. Creating your own templates is very easy. There are two main steps:

1. Create a new document in the usual way.
2. Save the document as a template, using the Save <u>A</u>s dialog.

Let's create a fax cover sheet and save it as a template for future use. We'll use a table to lay out the text on the page

🖱 *Create a new document using* 🔲.

🖱 *Insert a 5-row by 2-column table using* ▦. *You can add any extra rows you require later on.*

Adjust the size of the first column so that it is 1" wide

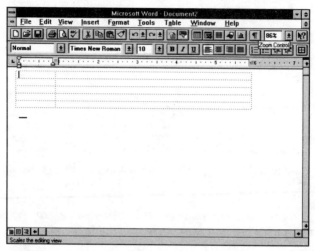

🖱 *Merge the two cells in the top row by selecting the cells and choosing T̲able Merge Cells.*

Type

Facsimile Enter

Acme Widget Co.

🖱 *Format it as Arial, 36pt, left aligned, with the company name in italics.*

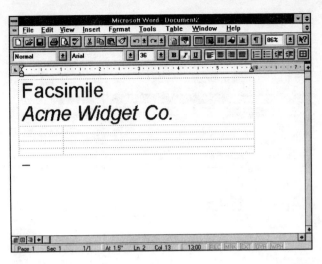

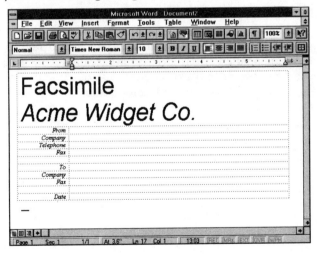

🖱 *Enter the rest of the text, using ⌨Tab to move to the next cell. Also use ⌨Tab to add a new row at the end of the table, if necessary.*

🖱 *Select the cells that will hold the label text (**From**, etc. in the first column). Right align and italicise them.*

Type **Message** *in the last cell and format it in the same way that* **Facsimile** *is formatted.*

Apply any borders and shading to the table using the Borders toolbar. Remember that the gridlines will not print.

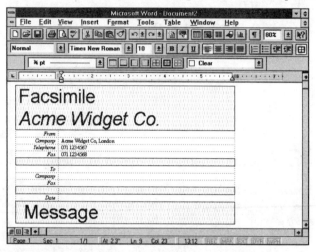

Saving the template

Having created the document, you will save it as a template. In general, you should ensure that there is nothing in the document that would be specific to a particular occasion, e.g. name or date. The template should contain only information that is used every time.

🖰 *Choose Save As... from the File menu.*

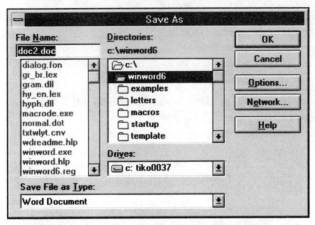

In order that Word can save this document as a template, change the Save File as Type to 'Document Template'.

Click the Save File as Type option and choose Document Template.

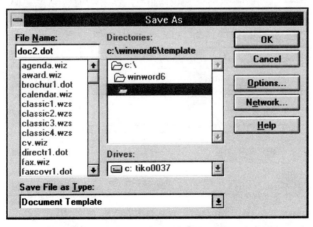

Note that Word has chosen the directory for you. When you save a template, the directory list is greyed out indicating that you cannot change it. In order for Word automatically to find a template and offer it on the list when you use the File New... command, the template must be stored in a specific template directory.

🖱 *Type a filename such as* MYFAX *and click* [OK]

If you have set up Microsoft Word to prompt you for summary information, the Summary Information dialog will be displayed.

🖱 *If the Summary Information dialog is not displayed, choose File Summary Info...*

The summary information is extremely useful when creating a template because the title line of the dialog is used as the description of the template in the File, New... dialog box.

🖱 *Enter the description for your template into the first line of the Summary Information dialog and click* [OK]

🖱 *If you had to use File Summary Info to display this dialog (i.e. if it was not offered automatically as part of the save process), save the template again.*

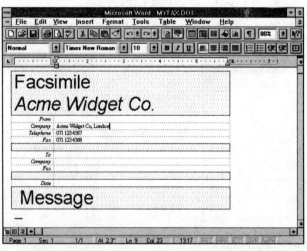

Notice that the title bar now reads MYFAX.DOT, the .DOT indicating that this is a document template.

🖱 *Close the file using File Close.*

You have already seen how to use a template when you used the MEMO1 template earlier. Your new template, MYFAX, behaves in exactly the same manner.

Choose File New... and select the template MYFAX.

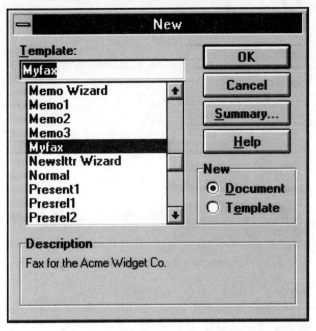

Notice that the description of this template is the same as the title
you typed in the summary information.

 *Click* OK

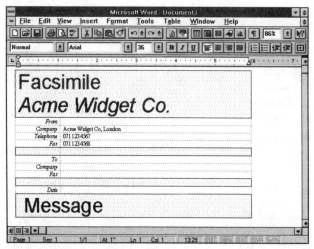

Word has created a new document based on the MYFAX.DOT template.

Summary: Templates

- A template is a 'blueprint' for a document, containing (amongst other things) a collection of styles and default text for the new document
- You access templates using File New.
- Word comes with a collection of prewritten templates.
- Word also provides wizards for writing letters, memos, etc. that guide you through the process in easy steps. Many wizards make use of templates.
- Creating a template is straightforward: create your document and style-set; then save it as a document template using the Save As dialog.

22

───── STYLES ─────

This chapter covers:

- The purpose of styles.
- The difference between character and paragraph styles.
- How to apply styles.
- How to define styles.
- The AutoFormat feature.

───── What are styles? ─────

In earlier chapters, you have looked at how to apply formatting to text. Often, you would apply the same set of formatting commands to a number of paragraphs or phrases. For example, you might have a standard look for all the headings in your document. Rather than having laboriously to apply each of the separate commands to every heading, it is possible to bundle them all together into a **style**. You can define a style to contain a number of formatting features, and then simply apply that style to the desired text. Each style is given its own unique name to identify it.

There are two obvious advantages of this: first, applying the formatting will be quicker; secondly, it is easier to make sure that all headings, say, have the same formatting features applied to them.

Applying a style to a piece of text does more than just change the formatting of that text: it 'tags' that text with the name of the style. This means that if you later change the definition of that style, all occurrences of the style in the document will change to reflect the new definition. This is a very important and powerful feature of styles.

Styles are not used just for headings, though. All text in a document has some style applied to it, even if this is just the 'normal' style for the document. You might define a style for the normal body text in your document, or define a style of text in tables, or forming part of a bulleted list. Any piece of formatting which you might need consistently applied throughout a document could be defined as a style.

Character styles and paragraph styles

When you looked at formatting, you saw that it could be divided into four main types: font, paragraph, section and document formatting. Styles can be used to apply the first two of these in a semi-automated manner. Thus, styles are divided into character styles and paragraph styles.

Paragraph formatting covers a wide range of formatting features available in Word: you can specify the font, indents, line spacing and borders for paragraphs using this form of style. Like paragraph formatting, the smallest block of text to which a paragraph style can be applied, is a paragraph.

Character formatting can be applied to single characters. It is possible for a character in a block of text to have two styles applied to it – a character style and a paragraph style. The types of formatting that can be included in a character style are more limited: it is mainly restricted to the features available in the F<u>o</u>rmat <u>F</u>ont dialog.

Direct formatting

When you looked at formatting before, you applied the formatting commands to the text itself. This is called **direct formatting**. Essentially, direct formatting overrides the formatting commands of the style underneath. Sometimes, this can be done without harm – for example, italicising a short phrase to highlight it. However, for changes that are going to affect the entire document, such as increasing the point size throughout, you should change the definition of the style rather than apply direct formatting.

Styles are designed to make these global changes. By applying direct formatting, you will prevent the full effect of any changes in the style definition from showing through.

☝ *Using* ❓, *you can see whether character and paragraph formatting have been affected by direct formatting.*

Returning to the style format

There are two simple keystrokes to help you remove any formatting applied to text:

`Ctrl` `Space` will revert highlighted text to the default paragraph font: it will remove any character styles applied, and remove any direct formatting.

`Ctrl` `Q` will reset any changes to the paragraph formatting – that is, indents, borders, or bullet points, etc. It will not reset changes to the font, such as bold, italics, or point size.

Where styles are stored

Styles can either be stored solely within the document they are created, or within a template. One of the main features of templates (which you looked at in the previous chapter) is that they provide a number of styles that can be used in documents based on that template.

Styles stored in a document will only be available for use within that document. Styles stored in a template are available in any document based on that template.

———————— Applying styles ————————

 Open the document SAMPLE7.DOC.

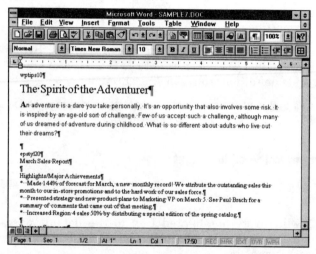

You have seen this document already: it is the example you used when you were looking at formatting. Here, you are opening the original version of this file again, which does not contain any of the changes you made to it in the earlier exercises.

The style box

The style box, at the front of the Formatting toolbar, can be used to quickly apply a pre-defined style. It will also show what style has been applied to the selected text. Paragraph styles appear in a bold face; character styles appear in a lighter face.

👍 *If both character and paragraph formatting have been applied to the selected text, then character formatting will override.*

🖱 *Scroll down to the top of page 2 of the document, and position your insertion point in the heading* **The Conductor.**

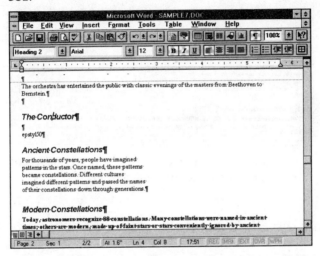

The style box displays the style which has been applied to this template: in this case, Heading 2 style. You can change this using the style box. Remember, all paragraphs have a style, even if it is only the normal style.

🖱 *Drop down the list of styles in the style box, and scroll up through the list until you see* **Heading** 1. *Select it.*

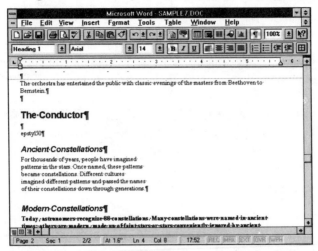

Clearly, the title is now bigger and in a slightly different style. You will try this again on a different paragraph.

Using the Style dialog to apply styles

🖱 *Move your insertion point to somewhere in the paragraph under the heading* **Ancient** **Constellations,** *and choose Format Style.*

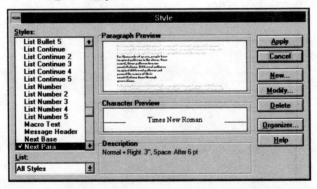

You will look at this dialog in more detail later, but for now:

Scroll through the list of styles on the left of the dialog and choose **Normal** *style.*

Click [Apply]

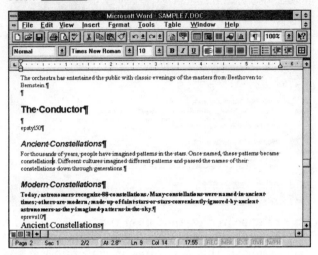

The indents on this paragraph are adjusted to fill the whole width of the page.

—————— Viewing the style area ——————

You have seen how the style box can be used to show which style has been applied to selected text. However, you can also get Word to show you which styles have been applied to each paragraph. Style names can be displayed in the style area. To show the style area, first make sure you are in normal view.

 Choose Tools Options, *then select the View Tab.*

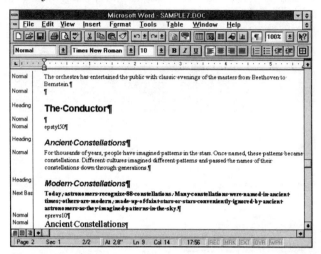

Set Style Area Width to 0.5"

A margin has appeared on the left of the screen. In it are the names of the styles being used, against the paragraphs to which they apply. If this style area is not quite the size you need it to be, you can resize it using the mouse:

Position your cursor over the line between the style area and the main document, so that your cursor becomes ╫.

🖰 *Click and drag the boundary so that you can see the full width of the style names without taking up too much screen space.*

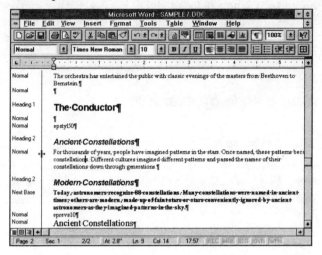

Note that it is the paragraph style only which appears in the style area.

—— Creating and modifying styles ——

When you create a new document, you will inherit a number of pre-defined styles (that were defined as part of the template your document was based on – often NORMAL.DOT). However, you may wish either to change these style definitions or to create totally new styles of your own. There are two general methods for doing this:

- **Style by example**, where you highlight a piece of text in the format desired, and define a style based on that selection; or

- **Using the dialog**, through Format Style... command, where you specify the format for a style using a number of other dialogs.

Which you use is largely a matter of preference. You may find that creating a style by example seems easiest at first — you build up the look of the text you require first, then assign a style name to it when it looks right. However, this method has its limitations (which will be discussed below). Using the dialog, it is possible to make more precise definitions of styles, and link them together.

Creating a style by example

🖰 *Move to the top of the document.*

You will create a new style based on the main heading for this document. First of all, you will make a few changes to it, so that it looks the way you want.

🖰 *Use the Formatting toolbar to change the heading* **The Spirit of the Adventurer** *to Arial, 20 point, bold and centred.*

🖰 *End with your insertion point placed somewhere within the heading.*

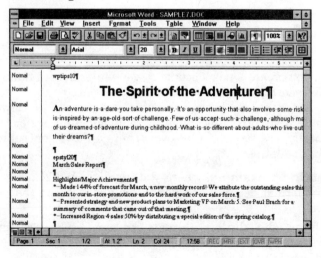

You will notice from the style area that, at the moment, this heading is still based on the Normal style although it has had some other formatting applied to it.

It is not necessary to select the whole paragraph, or any particular character within it: it is enough to put the insertion point somewhere within the text containing the desired formatting. This is because you will be creating a **paragraph** style.

Click the style box on the formatting toolbar, and type in the name of your new style: `Main Head`

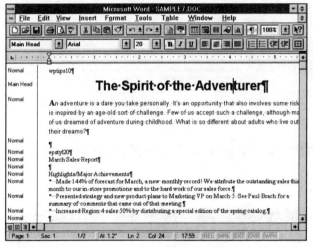

The style area now clearly shows that this heading is based on your new style. You can test out this style to prove that it works:

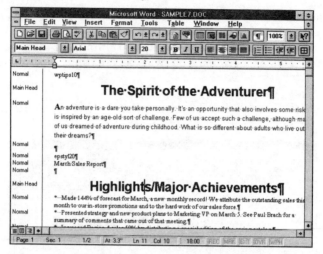

> Position the insertion point somewhere in the heading `Highlights/Major Achievements`. *Use the style box to apply* `Main Head` *style to it.*

Creating a style using the Format Style dialog

> Choose F<u>o</u>rmat <u>S</u>tyle...

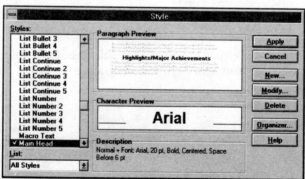

You have seen this dialog before. On the left of the dialog is a list of the styles in the document (precisely which styles are shown is controlled by the <u>L</u>ist feature beneath it). There will be a tick against two of the entries on this list, showing the character and paragraph styles currently in use. There are previews of the selected character and paragraph styles in the middle of this dialog, and a detailed description of the selected style at the bottom. You will return to this detailed description later.

To create a new style:

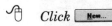 *Click* New...

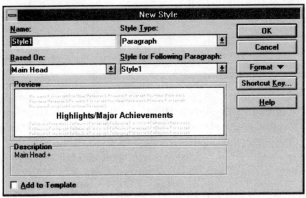

From this dialog, you specify the name and type of style you wish to create, and can move to other formatting dialogs to define the style. You will create a new character style for highlighting words.

In the Name field, type Important. *Under Style Type, set this to be a character style.*

Drop down the list under Based On.

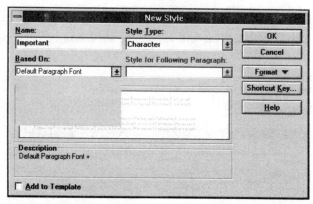

All styles (character or paragraph) are **based on** some other style. For paragraph styles, the default is the style called Normal. For character styles, the default is Default Paragraph Font. This concept of styles being based on other styles is quite important. In defining a new style, you effectively say how it differs from an existing style.

For example, you might define a heading style to be 'The same as the usual text, but in 16 point lettering.' In this case, you would define a heading style Based On whichever style was used in the body text. If you later changed the font used in the body text, the font used in the heading would also change; but, if you later changed the size of the body text, this would not be reflected in the heading, because the size of the lettering is defined in terms of how the heading differs from the body text.

With character styles, if you base them on the Default Paragraph Font, they will adopt whatever is in the Font part of the definition of the paragraph style of the text in which it will be placed. It will ignore any direct formatting that has been applied to the text.

Another option is to base the character style on a different character style. Do this if the link between the two styles is important.

 You will base your new style on Default Paragraph Font.

Since you will only be using this style in the current document, you will leave Add to Template cleared. If this box were to be checked, this style would be available in all other documents subsequently created from this template. Having set up the type of style this is, you must now define its 'look'.

 *Click* [Format ▼].

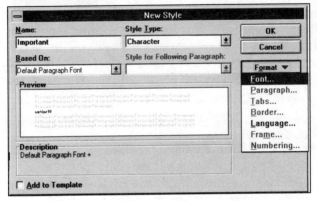

Most of these options are greyed out, because this is a character style.

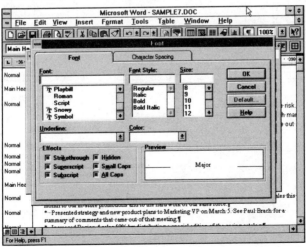 *Choose* Font

You should recognise this as the normal Font dialog (but notice, the New Style dialog can be seen behind it). You can now specify the font specifications for this style. Notice that there are no pre-existing settings in any of the fields — they are all blank. Unless you add settings to these fields, they will adopt those of the paragraph style of the text they are applied to (as described above).

The checkboxes also deserve some consideration. These appear initially in a 'neutral' state , which means 'don't care', they default to the paragraph style. Checkboxes here have three settings: checked, cleared, or neutral. To specify that a particular style will definitely be on or off, the checkbox must be checked or cleared.

Set the style to be Bold, All Capitals, and Red.

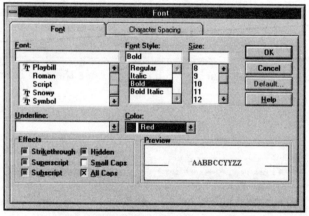

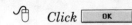 *Click* OK .

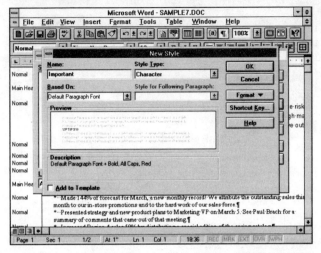

This takes you back to the New Style dialog. Notice the changes to the Description at the foot of this dialog.

At this point, it would be possible to assign a keystroke to this style using Shortcut Key... , which you could use instead of the other methods of applying styles already seen. In this case, it is not necessary.

Click OK *then* Close *to close all dialogs.*

Now, to test the new style:

Select the phrase **a new monthly record** *under the* **Highlights/Major Achievements** *heading.*

Use the style box to apply the Important style.

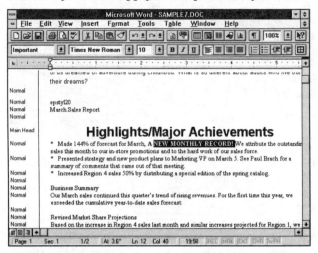

Modifying styles by example

Assume that you no longer like your Main Head style, and wish to change it. You can do this by altering one of the headings to which this style has been applied, then redefining the style to copy this example.

 Select the heading **The Spirit of the Adventurer** *again.*

Use the Borders toolbar to add a ¾ pt border around the heading. Also, make the heading right-aligned and in Times New Roman.

Making sure that the heading is still selected, use the style box to choose Main Head style again

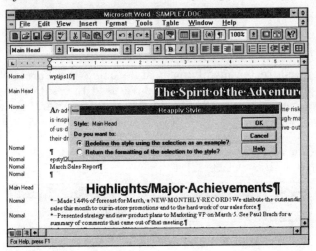

You are offered the choice of either removing all the direct formatting on the selected text and reverting to the style, or to redefine the style.

Ensure that ⊙ Redefine... is selected, and click **OK**.

Click somewhere else in the text to cancel the selection.

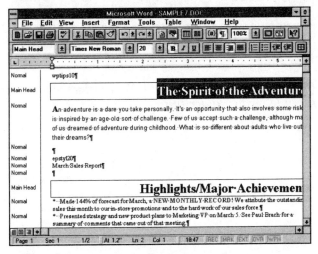

Notice that the Highlights/Major Achievements heading has also changed; it was also formatted in Main Head style.

Using the dialog to modify styles.

The procedure for modifying a style using the F*o*rmat *S*tyle command is similar to the procedure used to create the style. You will make some modifications to the 'Important' style you created earlier.

🖱 *Choose F*o*rmat S*tyle, *select the Important style from the list, and click* 〔 **Modify...** 〕*.*

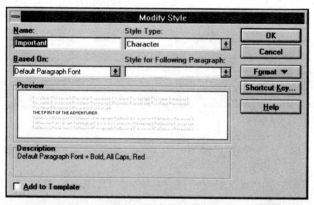

Notice here that you are no longer able to change the Style *T*ype. However, all other previously offered options are still available.

🖱 *Click* 〔 **Format ▼** 〕 *and choose Font. Change the style to green lettering, underlined.*

Close all the dialogs.

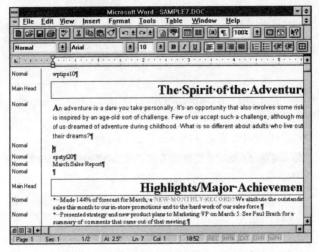

Again, notice that the change has been reflected in the text.

AutoFormat

Word provides ready-to-use styles for all documents. AutoFormat analyses the current document and applies those styles to each paragraph it deems appropriate.

AutoFormat can also

- Remove double paragraph marks used to leave blank lines, replacing them with a single paragraph mark, formatted to leave space after. This is a more flexible, and therefore preferable, approach to paragraph spacing.

- Apply 'smart' quotes (' ') instead of straight quotes (' ').

- Replace *, or other bullet-substitutes for real bullets e.g. •

- Indent paragraphs correctly, replacing tabs or spacebar indentation.

Applying AutoFormat

In order to test out the capabilities of the AutoFormat feature, you will close the current document without saving changes, then open it again (so as to discard the changes you made to it above.)

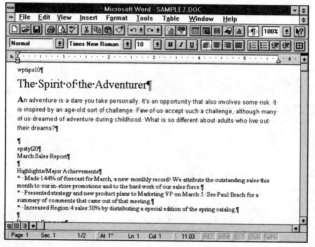

Close the current document. Do not save changes, when asked.

Then, open the file SAMPLE7.DOC again.

Note some of the things that are 'wrong' with this document: weak heading formatting, straight quotes ('), * used as a bullet symbol. At the end of the day these are matters of taste but documents formatted with strong headings tend to be more readable.

Click

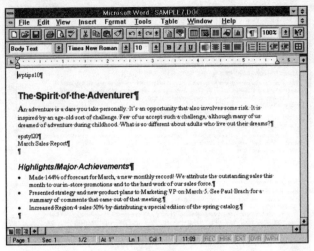

Note the changes that AutoFormat has made: headings are now formatted in a much stronger way; straight quotes have been replaced by smart quotes; the * bullets have been replaced with proper bulleted lists and double paragraph marks have been replaced by paragraph spacing.

However, not all formats are quite as you would like. For some reason the heading 'Ancient Constellations' at the bottom of page 2 has been missed:

Scroll down to the bottom of page 2.

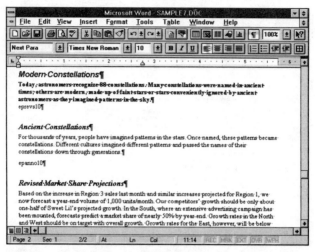

This illustrates another point: AutoFormat has to guess which paragraphs are meant to be titles, which are meant to be normal text and which are meant to be lists. It will not always get it quite right; however, the overall effect on this document is very effective. The point is not 'what went wrong?' but, 'how do you fine tune the formatting', because there will often be something that Word misinterprets.

The other problem is that some of the headings have not been formatted correctly:

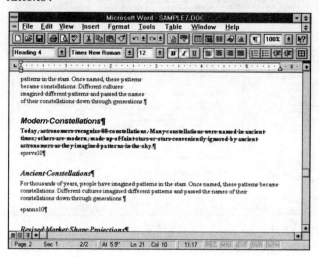

Move the insertion point to the heading 'Ancient Constellations'.

Clearly the heading 'Ancient Constellations' should be at the same level as the other headings.

The style gallery

Now that you have applied styles to your document you are able to reformat the document rapidly by using a different set of styles.

🖱 *Choose Style Gallery... from the Format menu.*

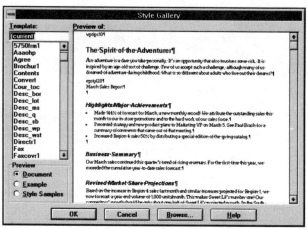

Presented here, on the left, is a list of current templates. One of the roles of templates is to store sets of styles. On the right is a preview of the document formatted in the current style-set.

🖱 *Click the template name Letter2 (you may have to wait a while to see the effect).*

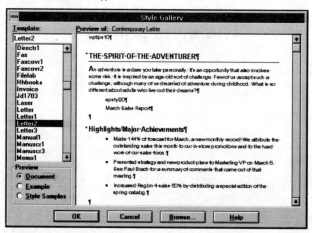

The preview has been redrawn using the style-set associated with the template Letter2.

🖱 *Try out some of the other templates.*

There are three preview options in the Style Gallery dialog:

◉ <u>D</u>ocument: previews current document formatted in this style.

◉ <u>E</u>xample: shows you an example document in this style.

◉ <u>S</u>tyle Samples: shows you the actual styles used.

Try using some of these options.

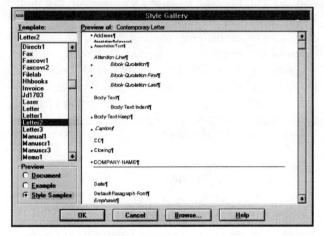

Finally, choose (current) from the top of the template list and click [**OK**] *to revert to the default template.*

Summary: Styles

- Styles can be used to apply multiple-format commands consistently to text throughout a document.
- Style information can either be stored in the document, or in a template.
- Paragraph styles contain all the formatting details about a paragraph, including fonts, indents, bullets, and borders.
- Character styles only contain font information, and can be used to highlight particular words or phrases.
- Changing the definition of a style will cause the formatting of all text using this style to change.
- Styles can be applied using the style box or the Format Style... dialog.
- Styles can be defined or modified using the Format Style dialog.
- Paragraph styles can also be defined or modified 'by example' using the style box.
- AutoFormat can be used to apply quickly pre-defined styles to your document.

APPENDIX 1
KEYSTROKES

This appendix will revise some useful keystrokes:

- `Ctrl` `A` means hold down `Ctrl` then press `A`
- Function keys are written as `F1` to `F10`

Typing things in	
`Enter`	Start a new paragraph
`Shift` `Enter`	Start a new line without starting a new paragraph
`Space`	Separate words

Moving through a document

→	Move one character to the right
←	Move one character to the left
↑	Move up one line
↓	Move down one line
End	Move to the end of a line
Home	Move to the beginning of a line
Ctrl →	Move one word to the left
Ctrl ←	Move one word to the right
Ctrl ↑	Move one paragraph up
Ctrl ↓	Move one paragraph down
PgUp	Move up one screen
PgDn	Move down one screen
Ctrl Alt PgUp	Move up one page
Ctrl Alt PgDn	Move down one page
Ctrl PgUp	Move to the top of a screen
Ctrl PgDn	and move to the bottom of the screen
Ctrl PgUp	Move to the end of a document
Ctrl PgDn	Move to the beginning of a document

Selecting text

Shift	With navigation keys, selects the text you move across
Ctrl A	Select the whole document
F8	Extend selection mode. Extend size of selection
Shift F8	Reduce size of selection

Deleting text	
`←Back`	Delete one character to the left of the insertion point; or if text has been selected, delete that text
`Ctrl` `←Back`	Delete one word to the left of the insertion point
`Del`	Delete one character to the right of the insertion point; or if text has been selected, delete that text
`Ctrl` `Del`	Delete one word to the right of the insertion point

Using the Clipboard	
`Ctrl` `X`	Cut selected text to clipboard
`Ctrl` `C`	Copy selected text to clipboard
`Ctrl` `V`	Paste contents of clipboard at insertion point

Undo and Redo	
`Ctrl` `Z`	Undo
`Ctrl` `Y`	Redo an action previously undone

Help	
`F1`	Help
`Shift` `F1`	Activate Help pointer

Character formatting

`Ctrl` `B`	Make text bold
`Ctrl` `I`	Italicise text
`Ctrl` `U`	Underline text
`Ctrl` `Shift` `W`	Underline words only (single underline)
`Ctrl` `Shift` `D`	Underline words only (double underline)
`Ctrl` `=`	Apply subscript text
`Ctrl` `+`	Apply superscript text
`Shift` `F3`	Change the capitalisation of words
`Ctrl` `Shift` `F3`	Change the font
`Ctrl` `Shift` `P`	Change the font size
`Ctrl` `Shift` `>`	Increase the font to the next available size
`Ctrl` `Shift` `<`	Decrease the font to the next available size
`Ctrl` `]`	Increase the font by 1 point size
`Ctrl` `[`	Decrease the font by 1 point size

APPENDIX 2
— INSTALLING —
WORD

This appendix covers:
- The system requirements for running Word
- The installation process

— System requirements —

In order to be able to run Word, your computer must meet certain minimum hardware and software requirements. Any less will not be powerful enough to run Word 6.

The minimum hardware your machine must have is as follows:

- An IBM PC or compatible, with an 80286, 80386, i486, Pentium or more powerful processor

- An EGA monitor, or some higher resolution compatible with Microsoft Windows, e.g. VGA.
- 4 MB of memory
- A hard disk with at least 5MB free (for a minimum installation of Word only)

The minimum software requirements are:

- MS-DOS operating system version 3.1 or later
- Any of the following versions of Microsoft Windows:
  - Windows 3.1 or later
  - Windows for Workgroups 3.1 or later
  - Windows for Pen Computing
  - Windows NT 3.1 or later

For full installation information, see later in this appendix.

The installation process

In this section, the method for installing Word on a normal, stand-alone computer will be detailed. It is possible to set up Word to run on a network, but that is beyond the scope of this book, and you are referred to the manual that comes with the software for more information on that.

Installing Word is a relatively simple process: the installation disks come with an automated installation program; all you have to do is make a few simple choices along the way. The installation process is conducted from within Windows. With Disk 1 of the set in drive A, it can be started:

- In File Manager, by double-clicking SETUP.EXE or;
- In Program Manager or File Manager by choosing File Run, then typing A:\SETUP

The installation program will check that your computer reaches the requirements for the software, and follows this with licensing agreements and then requests a location for the program.

The directory name tells you where the Setup program is going to put most of the Word files. Generally, you should not need to change this, but it is possible to do so using the Change Directory button. Otherwise, use [OK] to proceed with the installation.

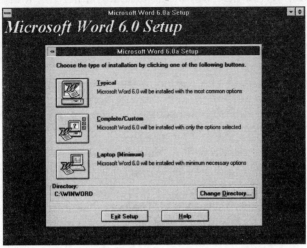

Word offers you three different levels of installation: Typical, Complete/Custom and Laptop.

- Typical installation installs those parts of Word used by the typical user. For every-day use of Word, and for the things covered in this book, a typical installation would be sufficient. This form of installation will require 18MB of free space on the hard disk of your computer.

- Complete/Custom allows you to pick which parts of Word you install. If you need to limit the amount of space taken up by Word, you may want to use this facility to pick exactly those features you require. A complete installation of Word requires 25MB of hard disk space.

- Laptop installation is a minimum installation — only those files deemed virtually essential to Word are installed on your machine. Since laptops usually have less hard disk space than other PCs, this minimum installation might be appropriate. A laptop installation requires 5MB of hard disk space.

When you choose a Custom/Complete installation, the next screen will allow you to specify which parts of Word you want to install. By clicking an option, you toggle between including it and excluding it. Towards the bottom of the dialog, there is a display of how much space the chosen installation will require, and how much is available.

After leaving this screen, you are asked whether you want to enable the special help system that comes with Word for WordPerfect users. You are also asked which Group in Program Manager you want the Word icons to appear in. Then, the installation process begins

A dialog appears in the corner of the screen, showing how far through the installation process you are, and what file is currently being processed. Information screens, in the top left of the screen, will occasionally appear, telling you about Word.

When all of the required files from this disk have been installed onto the hard disk, you will be prompted to insert the next disk in the series.

Replace the disk in Drive A with the next disk in the series, then click ⬚ OK ⬚. Continue in this manner until you have completed the installation.

—— Installation and examples ——

If you cannot find the *SAMPLE10.DOC* file in the ☐ *WORDCBT* directory then it is possible that you do not have a full installation of Word. If you need to install the sample files you will need 1.3MB of disk space and the Word for Windows installation disks numbered 1,2,7,8 and 9. To install only the sample files, run *SETUP.EXE* from the install disk 1 in drive A:. Word Setup checks for an existing version and when asked which setup option you require, choose **Add/Remove**. The Maintenance Installation begins. Ensure that **Examples and Demos** is selected and click ⬚ OK ⬚. Follow all the on-screen prompts to change disks and when complete you will have the sample files in the *C:\WINWORD\WORDCBT* directory.

INDEX